DYNAMICS OF SPIRITUAL WARFARE

DYNAMICS OF SPIRITUAL WARFARE

Biblical foundations for waging spiritual battles and for arresting demonic forces

Revised Edition

Nickson Banda

authorHOUSE®

AuthorHouse™
1663 Liberty Drive
Bloomington, IN 47403
www.authorhouse.com
Phone: 1-800-839-8640

First published by AuthorHouse 4/19/2010

ISBN: 978-1-4490-9320-4 (e)
ISBN: 978-1-4490-9319-8 (sc)

Library of Congress Control Number: 2010904833

Printed in the United States of America
Bloomington, Indiana

This book is printed on acid-free paper.

Scripture quotations in this book are from the New International Version.
Copyright © 1973, 1978, 1984, International Bible Society.

Scripture quotations identified KJV or NKJV are from the King James Authorised Version or the New King James Version of the Bible. Amp is the Amplified Bible.

Contact the author at ableinternet@gmail.com

About The Author

Nickson Banda is a spiritual warfare strategist, an apostolic teacher and a business consultant. He is a multi-gifted teacher of the Word and he functions widely in spiritual matters and economic affairs affecting communities. He has a strong interdisciplinary approach to life and his qualifications cuts across theology, conflict resolution, economics and business administration. He is the founder of Ambassadors of Change and Apostolic Mission's Network in South Africa. He is married to Mukonda and they together have two sons Israel Dexter and Nikao Daniel. He is an excellent communicator of truth and has attracted the attention of many denominations in many parts of the world. He has a passion for accurate apostolic patterns and Kingdom transformation through prophetic praying, intercession and spiritual warfare.

Dedication

In the first place I would like to acknowledge the Almighty God for His enabling power and grace for me to write this book. I dedicate this book to my lovely wife MUKONDA and to our two sons ISRAEL DEXTER and NIKAO DANIEL. Finally I encourage all intercessors, prayer warriors, Church leaders and all believers to use this material.

The greatest thing anyone can do for God and for man is to pray.
You can do more than pray after you have prayed, but you cannot
do more than pray until you have prayed.
(S.D. Gordon)

Table of Contents

Foreword

The subject of spiritual warfare is such an important one for every believer in Christ. A true Christian is a soldier, and as one engaging in a spiritual battle must of necessity be thoroughly knowledgeable concerning all that this warfare entails. Dr. Banda has made a diligent study of this vital subject and has painstakingly written this book providing us with valuable material. He has a burning desire to see believers in Christ mobilize and boldly confront this enemy of our souls and all his demonic forces with the sole purpose of defeating every advance made against God's people.

He has covered quiet a wide area in respect of this subject. The work reflects his experience, careful study, deep insight and a good understanding of the subject. The writing provides excellent resource material for those who are doing research on this topic. Prayer warriors and those who have studied this subject will do well to read this work and add to their fund of knowledge acquired by way of other readings on spiritual warfare. His powerful presentation is easy to understand and the language makes the contents of his writing easy to read and digest.

It gives me great pleasure to recommend this book to all who are eager to know more about real spiritual warfare. This publication is highly informative, educative and spiritually enriching. May all the readers find it most profitable in their encounter with the adversary and the demonic powers.

Dr. James D. Seekola
Senior minister, Full Gospel Church
Chatsworth, - Durban

Acknowledgements

This book has been made possible through prayer and support of all kind from concerned brothers and sisters in the Lord. It took both prayer and financial support to allow the successful completion and release of this book. The love and support from my wife Mukonda put me in a safe and secure position to write this book. The Lord used different men of God to **motivate, teach and inspire** me. These are Peter Wagner, Cindy Jacobs, Watchman Nee, George Otis Jr, Langton Gatsi, Dick Eastman, Larry Stockstill, Oswald Chambers, Clive Gopaul, John Pedersen, Dr. David Jonathan, Apostle Reginald Wilson sr, just to mention a few.

I appreciate Peter and Clara Marie Pedersen for being a great blessing in offering direction to us as a family. Thanks also to Apostle Asini and prophetess Annie Mwale of Kingsway Destiny Ministries who are also our parents in the faith. Thanks to Apostle Reginald Wilson and Pastor Vera Wilson for the support and guidance in the understanding of Kingdom matters. Thanks also to the willing support of sisters Betty Isaac and Betty McNeil in seeing that this edition is a success. May the Lord bless you all for your wonderful support? To Gerry and Author House, thanks for your great work. To those I have not enlisted here, just know that I appreciate you and I am fully aware of your support.

Introduction

Life in general is a fight and only those with the courage to fight will make it. We fight at all levels of experience and existence. Jesus told His disciples that "in this world you shall have trouble but be of good heart because I have overcome the world[1]. Our survival on earth is based on the victory of Christ because He is the One that has and will always overcome the evil one. Spiritual warfare allows the believer to fight at the highest level of his/her life. This book attempts to identify effective spiritual warfare strategies and to bring out an exposition of satanic operations and the world of demons. Peter Wagner[2] of the United Prayer Track of the AD 2000 & Beyond Movement said, "God is asking His people to rise up in even more serious prayer than they have previously attempted. The powers of darkness have kept huge numbers of people in captivity long enough and only prayer can break the chains of spiritual bondage and free millions upon millions of souls to hear and receive the gospel of Jesus Christ." It is through the knowledge of spiritual warfare that we can all occupy the position of actualizing the victory over the Luciferian advancements.

John Piper[3] writes that we cannot know what prayer is for until we know that life is war. Indeed it is war but how we fight this war is of primary importance. The reality of spiritual warfare is that we contend for our own souls by fighting demonic systems and strongholds that also seek the same soul.

Spiritual warfare in reality is a position we occupy to face the enemy at present for the purpose of allowing the Lord's victory in our lives. It is engaging the enemy (the devil) in a spiritual fight with spiritual words that can only be uttered by those who understand God's language. Spiritual warfare is also strategic prayer addressing the schemes and tactics of the devil through the powerful name of our Lord Jesus Christ.

True spiritual warfare is the position we occupy in prayer to fight the advancements of the invisible and visible forces of the enemy

In spiritual warfare, we contend and agonize intensely with both invisible and visible forces of darkness that opposes the will of God in our lives here on the earth. To ignore this fact is tantamount to denying the existence of Satan. I write this book being fully aware of the levels of demonic resistance and conflict around those who wrote the Bible. It is a deception to

---

[1]   John 16:33
[2]   Prayer Track News, 1999, Volume 8, N0 3: page 1
[3]   John Piper, 1993, Let the Nations be Glad, pp 45: Grand Rapids.

think spiritual warfare does not exist. The unawareness and denial of the practice of spiritual warfare by some believers has resulted into having more casualties and victims in the Church. It is through knowing the enemy that we can develop effective strategies to overcome him.

For one to be able to do spiritual warfare the following foundational requirements must be present:

1. Acknowledge that the devil is there.
2. Recognize the existence of evil spirits.
3. Christian life is a life of battles.
4. It is fully biblical to do spiritual warfare.
5. God has created us to rule with Him in the heavenly places.

The book of Revelation (12:12), the second part of the scripture says; "woe to the earth and the sea because the devil has gone down to you! He is filled with fury, because he knows that his time is short." Just by reading this, we should all know and acknowledge that the devil is very much around us and he is not just around us. He is filled with anger after losing his place in heaven and now he is the one who leads the whole world astray.[4] To ignore this plain truth just worsens things. People perish for lack of knowledge.

Spiritual warfare is simply the means through which we can defeat Lucifer just as he was defeated in that heavenly war[5]. The book of Revelation (12:10) confirms that 'Defeating the devil creates the platform for salvation, power, God's Kingdom and the authority of Christ to manifest to other people. The devil generally blinds the minds of unbelievers and to defeat him is to make light to shine in the minds of many people.

Effective spiritual warfare requires a good spiritual platform. It is highly concerned with our stand, conduct and the proclamation of the gospel to the dying world.

Let me underscore two important realizations for waging effective and biblically driven spiritual warfare. The first is basically *"how"* we fight this war or what type of climate is conducive for spiritual warfare. The climate for a good spiritual warfare happens under the following conditions:

- **Under Christ**, our Captain and champion who has all power (Heb 2:10). He is our banner (Ps 60:4). It is our submission to Christ that determines the level of victory we can sustain in our lives.

- **With faith** (1Timothy 1:18, 19) – it is impossible to please God without faith. Prayer and faith takes us into the realm of doing the impossible.

---

[4]   Revelation 12:9
[5]   Revelation 12:7-14

- **With a good conscience** (1Timothy 1:18, 19). Faith and a good conscience go hand in hand. Believers are required to have a sense of what is right or wrong which often comes from ethics and righteous principles.

- **With earnestness** (Jude 1:3) - Apostle James prayed from a position of gravity, seriousness and intensity. Spiritual warfare requires the fervency of the spirit and the determination to push for results.

- **With watchfulness** (1Corinthians 16:13; 1Peter 5:8). We are urged in scripture to pray and watch and to be vigilant. This is what determines the difference between victims and victors in life. Spiritual casualties are mainly due to lack of watchfulness (spiritual alertness). War generally requires the participants or combatants to be very watchful of their opponents.

- **With endurance of hardness** (2Timothy 2:3, 10). We are living in perilous and dangerous times. True spiritual soldiers know how to endure the suffering. Since spiritual warfare has the possibility of arousing fierce forces against those who engage the enemy, it is necessary that they learn to endure as Christ endured.

- **With self-denial** (1Corinthians 9:25-27). Everything about victory for a Christian has to do with self. One of the primary reason they conquered Lucifer[6] is 'they did not love their lives so as to shrink from death.' Self denial is death to self through a self giving experience.

- **With all kinds of prayer** (Eph 6:18). Though a single genuine prayer can bring results, it is not enough in a constantly changing society. Experiencing prayer at other levels (thanksgiving, petition, and penitential, intercessory) is always the best way of waging spiritual warfare.

- **Without earthly entanglements** (2Timothy 2:4). Spiritual things are always sustained by obedience and the spiritual commitment that goes with it. You cannot cast out the devil if the same devil is in you. Demons don't cast demons. Earthly entanglements for believers create an opportunity for the devil to attack. This is why we are not to give a foothold[7] to the devil.

- **Attack and defend combination** (2Corinthians 6:7). When threat and opposition was mounting up during the rebuilding of the wall in the book of Nehemiah the fourth chapter, those who carried materials did their work with one hand and held a weapon on the other hand and all builders wore their swords as they worked. In other words, they were building and fighting at the same time[8]. They were serious and they gave no chance to the enemy. Many Christians become casualties after attacking the devil simply because they do not have enough personal support and spiritual defense structure to expel the attacks.

---

[6]   Revelation 12:11
[7]   Ephesians 4:27 - NIV
[8]   Read Nehemiah 4:17 - 18

Experience has taught me a principle called "take cover" which is mostly used in military battle fields to caution the fighting solders about proximity and intensity of the fire shorts from the enemy.

The second realization is *"who"* to fight or the target of our warfare. The authority Christ has given the Church in spiritual warfare is to be exercised over the following:

1. Over the devil (Rom 16:20; 1John 2:14).
No doubt the devil is the man behind all demonic advances unleashed upon the earth. He is called the god of this world and the evil one. He is the man we need deliverance from (deliver us from the evil one). Though we cannot annihilate him for now, we have authority to resist his advances and even destroy his works (1 John 3:8).

2. Over the flesh (Romans 7:24, 25; Galatians 5:24).
The threefold temptations of man are the devil, the flesh and the world. The flesh has its own works and it lusts after the things of this world. Man is tempted by his own sinful desires because of his fleshly nature. Christians should always learn to crucify the flesh.

3. Over the world (1John 5:4,5).
It is clear in the Word of God that friendship with the world is enmity with God. The world and its systems are in themselves a battle ground. Unless believers learn to overcome the world, spiritual warfare will become a difficult experience. Obedience is the only power strong enough to punish disobedience.[9]

4. Over all that exalts itself against the knowledge of God (2Corinthians 10:5).
We wage war against ideologies, philosophies, pretensions, theories and concepts that seek to defy and deny the truth about God. Worldviews such as animism and western worldview are some of the platforms where man wants to exalt himself above the knowledge of God. It is in this realm that we demolish strange strongholds that have established themselves in the minds of the people.

5. Over death and the grave, sicknesses (Isaiah 25:8; 26:19; 1Corinthians 15:54, 55).
Spiritual warfare also has to do with taking authority over sickness and disease. Through the power of Him that rose from the dead, we too by the Holy Spirit have the power to defeat the grave and to declare victory over all the works of the enemy.

6. Over demonic establishments and strongholds (Jer1:10; 2 Cor 10:4).
Today's society is characterized by a lot of demonic establishments or thrones in various forms and shapes. The category ranges from satanic temples, masonic lodges, shrines, dedicated buildings, writings, placards, traditional healing centers using fetishism, disco houses and brothels, prostitution houses, sex clubs and many more.

---

[9]   Read 2 Corinthians 10: 6 - NIV

CHAPTER ONE

INTRODUCTION TO SPIRITUAL WARFARE

The Need for Spiritual Warfare

Ignorance and wrong theological influence and conclusions have caused many to deny the reality of spiritual warfare. I have met people who are non Christians coming to see me that there seeing forces of darkness during their sleep attacking them and they would want me to pray for them. I have also prayed for religious leaders who completely deny the existence of spiritual warfare but have had encounters with demonic powers. These examples just show that many people do experience the reality of demonic forces in their lives but they deny the reality of it until they are in deep trouble. One atomic scientist admitted some years ago that 'prayer is the mightiest force in the universe.' No statement could be more accurate.

If the heavenly hosts engaged Lucifer in war that broke out in heaven[10]where Lucifer was defeated and hurled down to the earth, how much more warfare should we expect here on earth considering that Lucifer is fuming with anger of losing his place in heaven? Scripture confirms that the devil is on a war mission with those who obey God's command and hold to the testimony of Jesus (Revelation 12:17).

If living a Christian life has nothing to do with spiritual warfare, then a lot of scriptures including the ones below must be removed from the Bible. There is probably more spiritual warfare in the Bible than any other subject. The word battle appears 230 times in scripture and the word fight appears 200 times. Perhaps the scripture below will shade more light on why we very much need to practice spiritual warfare.

Ephesians 6:11 and 13 (AMP)

V11

> *"Put on God's whole armor (the armor of a heavy – armed soldier which God supplies), that you may be able successfully to stand up against all the strategies and the deceits of the Devil."*

---

[10]   Revelation 12: 7 - 12

V13

"Therefore put on God's complete armor, that you may be able to resist and stand your ground on the evil day (of danger)) and, having done all (the crisis demands), to stand (firmly in your place)."

The above verses communicate the need for preparation in relation to danger, evil day, and in times of crisis. By implication, there is a warfare that awaits every child of God here on earth. The key to wage this war is to possess the right spiritual attire (dressed for war) that will enable us to fight the enemy regardless of the day he comes. Remember the devil is like a roaring lion seeking whom to devour. The enemy always comes when we least expect him and he attacks when we underestimate his power.

We have to wrestle with the devil's power, to resist it all, to stand against everything in the confession of Christ, of the light; we have to do all that the confession of His name requires in spite of all and at whatever cost, and to be found standing when the storm and the evil day are past.

Though the Church is on the winning side, the question of what to fight, who to fight, why fight and when to fight" is very important in spiritual warfare issues.

The subject of spiritual warfare has been so obvious in my own life. In the early times of my acquaintance with spiritual warfare, I knew that I needed to prepare for warfare at another level higher than an average Christian. So I began to prepare myself adequately for spiritual warfare encounters. At this time of my life, very few people were authorities in the field of spiritual warfare. In not less than a year I realized the need for spiritual warfare. Much of it came by looking into the Word of God. I was able to do constructive practical spiritual warfare in my community. Many people were blessed of what I was doing. I knew certainly that the Lord was asking me to increase the passion for spiritual warfare. So I began to associate myself with key spiritual warfare leaders in Africa and outside Africa. My view and knowledge of the subject was expanding greatly and I began to write something in the same lines.

Much of my involvement in spiritual warfare apart from my personal walk with God was practical and onsite. The whole process was not easy because of many dangers that I ended up encountering in spiritual warfare situations. I realized that spiritual warfare was not for the weak or the ignorant. So I began to learn the dynamics of spiritual warfare both from the Bible and from experience. I must add that, if you cannot pray when you are alone, you will never sustain a spiritual warfare breakthrough. Having grown in the knowledge of spiritual warfare, I knew then what to do and what not to do. It is from here that I could get these dynamics and compile them together. This is what the book is all about. If we cannot learn the dynamics of spiritual warfare, it will be too hard for us to overcome the enemy. Spiritual warfare is built on a strong foundation of person conduct and relationship with the Lord. The approach I have taken in this study can be applied in any part of the world although situations may differ from place to place. We cannot manage to defeat the devil just by binding and loosing alone. By the way the devil is not very scared of binding and loosing. He is threatened more by our position in the Lord than when we are just religiously praying.

Jesus in **Matthew 16:19** spoke to Peter something we cannot afford to miss. He said, "**I will give you the keys of the kingdom and whatever you bind on earth shall be bound in heaven and whatever you loose on earth shall be loosed in heaven.**" The first part of this verse (I will give you the keys) is what we all need to possess higher levels of victory over every demonic situation. We need the **keys of the Kingdom** first before we can do the binding and the loosing. The advantage of having the key is that, you don't have to knock before you enter. All you need to do is to identify the right door and open the door with your keys and go in. The KEYS of the Kingdom takes us straight into the Kingdom of God where we can get every navigational tool or principle that we can use in this life.

The doors of victory God will open for us in life are determined by the type of keys we obtain from Him.

In the Kingdom of God, authority emanates from the King and the Christians are the beneficiaries of the royal table. The keys of the Kingdom are established divine principles that give us access into all Kingdom business. Having the keys means we can open doors without struggling. If you are serious about getting the right keys, ask God to give you as He did to Peter. In spiritual warfare, we all need divine keys to open doors of victory.

To neglect the subject of spiritual warfare is to make ourselves vulnerable to demonic attacks. What God expects in every Christian is 100% victory over the works of the devil – in fact that's the reason for the manifestation of the Son of God **(1 John 3:8b)**. The works mentioned here in scripture refers to operations, schemes, practices, and activities of the devil. The devil's aim has always been to steal, kill and to destroy. These three words describe how really the devil is and how intense the Christian battle is. The devil has been using every tactic, every weapon and diabolical strategy to hinder Christians from being effective. His specific strategies are there or plotted to keep the Church in a weakened position. The Church must realize that, to give life to this wicked generation involves fighting because the devil wants to "kill" and "destroy" the same life.

To Ignore the Devil Is To Invite Him In

History of the Old Testament teaches us that the Israelites went through so many battles before they could finally enter the Promised Land. Jesus lived a life of battles before He could win the world to Himself. The early Church apostles encountered strong demonic resistance and fierce opposition before they could be known for miraculous works. All these people acknowledged and recognized the existence of the enemy. Now is the time for every true child of God to rise up with the God given authority to take position and fight. We are equipped with divine spiritual authority to overcome all the power of the enemy. According to Luke 10:19, we have been given authority to trample on snakes and scorpions, and to overcome all the power of the enemy and nothing will harm us.

*There's absolutely no demonic power that can stand
God's dynamic power in every child of God*

A society we are in today is filled with conflict, fear, wars, generations battling generations, generations warring within themselves. What we see here is that the seeds of the enemy have been planted and are ready to spring forth unless urgent, fervent prayer is released. The Church is being prepared to approach each year with an overcoming spirit and a breakthrough mentality. God's power in those who believe is strong enough to break down every demonic resistance. But if Christians are not prepared enough to take the right position of authority boldly, then we are on our way to receiving more victims and casualties in the body of Christ."

Our God is a victory oriented God. He is All Powerful. When the devil uses stratagems to fight us, we have to use strategies to fight him back. But before we fight, we must be equipped and anointed for battle. Any military group that wants to engage warfare today takes serious training; knows how to handle and use weapons, puts on uniform and then always ready to fight when the enemy strikes. Often times men of God say, "failure to prepare is preparation for failure." So it is a prepared generation of Christians that will do the work of spiritual warfare.

What Is Spiritual Warfare

The subject of spiritual warfare must not be confused with spiritual welfare because the two are not the same. What John talks about in **3 John verse 2** is **spiritual welfare.** Spiritual warfare is implied and best reflected in **Ephesians 6: 12 (NIV).**

Verse 12

> *"For our struggle is not against flesh and blood, but against the rulers,*
> *against the authorities, against the powers of the dark world and*
> *against the spiritual forces of evil in the heavenly realm."*

Other translations use the 'wrestle' instead of the word struggle. Wrestle is the Greek noun *Pale*, it carries the idea of a contest between two enemies in which each endeavors to throw the other, and which is decided when the victor is able to hold his opponent down with his hand upon his neck. The term is transferred to the Christian's struggle with the power of evil. This is without doubt talking about spiritual warfare.

The other word that points us to spiritual warfare is the word '**against.**' It appears five times in the above passage. The word 'against' comes from a Greek word '*pros.*' It is the strengthened form of a Greek preposition '*pro*' which means, '**in front of, superior to.**' The word '**pros**' would therefore mean, '**forward to, accusation unto, motion towards, facing forward or stepping forward.**'

One of the ideas of the **Ephesians 6:12**, is that of a wrestler facing or making motion towards his opponent. In this case we are making motion towards obstacles and satanic forces of different levels of influence.

It is as if God is saying to the Church, "**Step forward, go in front and face the powers of darkness.**" The concept of battlefront comes from the same idea. We are to aggressively and forcefully deal with the forces of darkness whenever we encounter them especially by our conduct and in the way of the gospel. When David showed up to face Goliath, the Bible records that he ran quickly to the battle line to meet Goliath.[11]

Our enemies according to Ephesians 6:12 are principalities and powers-beings possessing an energy of evil which has its source in a will that has mastery over those who do not know how to resist it; they have also strength to carry it out. These are powers that have forsaken God; the spring of their actions is in their own will. These rebellious principalities and powers rule over the darkness of this world. Light is the atmosphere in which God dwells, which He diffuses all around Himself. Wicked spirits deceive and reign in darkness. Now this world, not having the light of God, is entirely in spiritual darkness, and demons reign in it; for God is not there-except in supreme power after all, turning everything to His glory, and, in the end, to the good of His children.

But if these principalities rule in the darkness of this world they do not possess merely an outward force; they are in the heavenlies, and are occupied with spiritual wickedness there. They exercise a spiritual influence, as having the place of gods. There is then, first, their intrinsic character, their mode of being, and the state in which they are found; second, their power in the world as governing it; and third, their religious and delusive ascendancy, as lodging in the heavens. They have also, as a sphere for the exercise of their power, the lusts of man, and even the terrors of his conscience.

We are called to step forward and realize the victory God has given us.

Spiritual warfare is …..

- War with the Luciferian systems determined by the devil where believers engage in a spiritual fight with the powers of darkness in the spiritual realm **(Rev. 12: 7).**
- Multilevel contest with demonic forces operating in darkness initiated on the supernatural plane and transferred onto the natural plane.
- Extending the Kingdom of God through the process of fighting and possessing the gates of the enemy **(Matthew 16:13; Gen. 22:17).**
- Engaging the invisible forces in the spiritual realm through a violence process of advancing into the enemy's territory **(Matt.11: 12; Joshua 6:1-6).**
- A combination of the inward and outward struggles against the world and its fleshly and sinful desires.
- War with invisible forces behind every visible demonic throne or rulership at different levels of life **(Eph 6: 12).**

---

[11] 1 Samuel 17:48 - NIV

- Positioning oneself in the place of battle to fight or wrestle with the forces that continually oppose God's will on earth (**Psalm 110: 2**).
- War against forces that work vigorously to thwart God's work on earth. The forces behind the revolt are unseen, non physical, and supernatural.

Jack Hayford says,
"There is a way to face impossibility. Invade it, not with speaking positive words, not in anger, not through self control. Invade impossibility with violence."

This is not violence of human strength against spiritual enemies. It is being violent in prayer and intercession (unceasing prayer) and in applying the authority Christ has given us. That's the only way we can see spiritual warfare manifesting itself. We are to fight a fight of faith.

Understanding of Demonic Activities

Understanding of demonic activities and satanic operations must be a primary step before taking up any spiritual warfare situation. As we know him (the devil) we learn how to defeat him. Even though Satan id defeated, he still rules this world through a hierarchy of demons who tempt, accuse and deceive those who fail to put on the armor of God.[12] Apostles knew the devil and because they knew him, they closed all the doors he could use to get to them.

Paul in **2 Corinthians 2:11 says (KJV)**
"Lest Satan should get an advantage of us, for we are not ignorant of his devices."

AMP: Says,
> *"To keep Satan from getting the advantage over us, for we*
> *are not ignorant of his wiles and intentions"*

In the above scripture, we are urged not to be ignorant (unaware) of Satan and his tactics. Ignorance is really costly. The devil takes advantage of the ignorant. The word ignorant in the above verses is the Greek word '*Agnes*' – it means ....

- **Inability to know due to lack of information or intelligence.**
- **By implication it means, "to ignore through disinclination**
- **Without understanding or knowledge.**
- **Failure to know and acknowledge the truth**

So the knowledge of the enemy is directly linked to the attacks of the enemy on our lives. Satan takes full advantage of those without the understanding of his schemes and ways. Let me also explain few other words that will help shape the nature of the devil's tactics.

The word 'device' or scheme is the Greek word '*noema.*' It means, 'thought, minded, device or intellect dispositions.' In other words, the verse above implies that, "don't be without

---

12   Neil T. Anderson, 2001, the steps to freedom on Christ, Ventura, Regal Books: Page 4

understanding or knowledge of what the devil thinks or has in his mind." We can only know what the devil has in mind by studying his purpose, plans, plots and schemes as revealed in scripture. It is imperative for us to know the moves of the devil if we are to engage him in war.

The word 'wiles' is the Greek word '*methodeia*'which means, **tricks, methods, traveling over.** Again we are challenged to possess a great deal of knowledge of the tricks, methods and moves of the devil. The devil targets mostly those who are unaware of his schemes and encroachments. That's why the Bible says; he is looking for someone or whom to devour.

Ephesians 6:12 gives us the angelic organization or the classes of demons. (NIV)

> *"For our struggle is not against flesh and blood, but against the principalities, against the authorities, against the powers of this dark world and against the spiritual forces of evil in the heavenly realm."*

A brief satanic organization.

1. **Satan – (Lucifer, the dragon, the devil Rev 12:7 – 9).**
2. **Principalities** – chief rulers or princes over nations.
3. **Authorities** – Area rulers, mediums of demonic activities.
4. **Powers** – binding abilities enforcing bandages.
5. **Wicked forces in the heavenly places** – Evil altars and reigning demonic high places.

Purpose of Spiritual Warfare

The purpose of spiritual warfare must be understood completely or else battles will be fought for nothing. Failure to understand the purpose of spiritual warfare is to defeat the whole essence of spiritual warfare. Below are the purposes of spiritual warfare or the main reasons why Christians are engaged in a continuous war with the enemy.

(I) To drive people to the likeness of Christ.

The very first reason for spiritual warfare is to allow Christ to be formed in people. We overcome the devil and sin so as to invite the Lord in our situation. In spiritual warfare, we don't fight to show that we have defeated the devil or to know that we are strong. Today, thousands of Christians all over the world are waging war for one thing – '**the transformation of human life so that God's Kingdom can be established in the hearts of many people.**' Jesus said, "Rejoice not because the demons are submitting to you but that your name is written in the book of life."[13] Spiritual warfare is for getting people into the Kingdom of God. Jesus overpowered the enemy so as to save those that were held captive by the devil. We are waging war so as to usher people to God. Jesus' ministry in Mark 10: 45 and the reason behind His earthly battles were for the **transfer of people from captivity to Christianity.** Taking the thought further, Jesus openly declared the building of His Church in Matthew

---

[13]   Luke 10:20 - NIV

16:18 and that the gates of hell shall not prevail. Gates of hell signifies how Satan has kept people bound with the chains of sin locked up in a place called darkness. Jesus by saying I am building my Church is implying that, He is advancing His attacks towards hell because His mission to call those in darkness out of spiritual darkness. This is why He sat and ate with sinners. The term Church is the Greek word *Ekklesia* which means 'people called out' or 'the called out ones.' Jesus came to seek and save the lost. The truth is that sinners are locked up in the chains of darkness unless the prayer warriors are willing to break the gates of hell. Jesus by addressing the gates of hell was also saying, unless we face the gates of the enemy and stop him from blinding people, we will never build the Church. Satan may think he has them all but the truth is God has power to deliver the people He died for. In spiritual warfare we are to make every thought obedient to Christ **(2 Corinthians 10:6).**

(II) To promote a free and holy relationship between man and God**.**

Man right from the Garden of Eden to this very point in time has been the target of the devil. The devil survives by attacking man. He (the devil) roars like a lion seeking whom to devour (1 **Peter 5: 8).** Therefore, for mankind to have a good relationship with God, spiritual warfare is a must. Paul confessed of being hindered by Satan (**1 Thessalonians 2:18**) from seeing the brethren he longed to see. Only the devil can disturb man's relationship with the Lord. We wage war so we can enhance our relationship with the Lord.

(III) To expose and disarm Satan and his weapons

Whenever the devil is not noticed, he gets happy and keeps his weapons hidden. Only the prayers of the saints bring confusion into his territory. Powerful and targeted intense prayers will always expose the devil. We must expose him for people to easily identify his true colors so that he doesn't hide anymore. What Jesus did on the cross was to disarm the powers and authorities, making a public spectacle of them and triumphing over them all.[14]

(IV) To advance God's Kingdom on earth.

One of the reasons why we should fight is to possess as many areas as we can for the Lord (**Psalm 2:8**). The more we evict demons from certain areas, the more responsive people will become to the Word of God in those same areas. In the end many people will come to the Lord (**Matt 6:10).** God's will to be done here on earth should be the primary concern of every believer. Because the devil is the god of this world, it will not be an easy job to establish the Kingdom of God here on earth. One important realization for believers in support of this truth is to recognize the fact that, the Kingdom of God truly suffers violence or has been forcefully advancing and only forceful men will take hold of it. Spiritual warfare will help us achieve this mission.

(V) To experience divine breakthrough in this wicked generation.

---

14   Colossians 2:15 - NIV

Every child of God needs a breakthrough in one area or another. In **Daniel 10:13–20,** Daniel became a breakthrough believer through the intensity of prayer and spiritual warfare. The battle was won in the closet. Jesus while on earth fasted and prayed earnestly and intensely. The writer of Hebrews records that Jesus prayed with loud cries and tears.[15]

Jesus one time challenged the disciples on the need for intensive warfare. They tried to cast out the demons but they failed, and they wondered at the situation until Jesus made it clear to them of the need for them to engage higher levels of fasting and prayer.

(VI) To prepare Christians for spiritual battles.

Immediately after Paul's introduction of the Christian war in **(Ephesians 6:12)**, he goes on in verse thirteen with the caution of the need for Christians to prepare for warfare. Thank God today at least most of the people in the Church now understands the importance of preparation before doing anything in the Kingdom of God. After having suffered many attacks from the enemy, the Church is now prepared to fight back and take back what belongs to her. We need to tear down, uproot and destroy the works of the enemy. (Jeremiah 1:10; 2 Corinthians 10: 5). This is another level of spiritual warfare dealing specifically with demonic strongholds and territorial spirits.

(VII) To protect Christians from the attacks and plots of the enemy

For the Church to remain protected in this wicked generation, spiritual warfare is a necessity **(Eph 6: 13; Matthew 26: 41).** Prayer as a powerful force has got power to stop all the missiles of the enemy.

Our protection lies in God, but it has to be appropriated by prayer and dependence on God in times of trouble **(James 5:13)**. Our strength is in the Lord and in the power of His might **(Ephesians 6:10).**

(VIII) To Restore the Bride of Christ

The Church is the bride of Christ and God's mandate in dealing with demonic forces is to restore the bride to her rightful place. According to **(Joel 2: 25)**, spiritual warfare helps us to restore what the enemy has stolen from the Church. We have to make the devil pay back what he has taken and eaten from the Church. We should possess all that which belongs to Christ and enforce the defeat on the devil. God's plan of crushing Satan has also to do with restoring the Church to her perfect position.

The Church and Spiritual Warfare.

The word 'Church' is a Greek word - *Ekklesia* - **(Ek–klay - see'-ah)** meaning, '**the called out ones**' or '**the assembly of saints**' **(set apart ones)**. So the Church is not a specific building or a religion of some kind but **the assembly of saints who are set apart to God**. 'Called

---

[15]   Hebrews 5:7

out ones' refers to those whom Christ Has called to Himself - hence, the "Body **of Christ.**" Today we call the 'called out ones' as **believers,** because they have believed in Him who has called them. God has called the Church out of darkness to be His. He has chosen the Church to be the means through which He can accomplish His purposes on earth. Believers are given the place of rulership with Christ in the heavenly places. Since the Church is the platform through which Christ can engage the earth, the devil's plan is to destroy the Church so he can hinder God's plan from coming through. Apostle Paul before his conversion tried vigorously to destroy the Church but he failed. He was only persecuting the Church by raising murderous threats against the disciples (Acts 9:1, 21). A true Church set up and built up by God is in continuous war with the enemy. But as Christ is lifted up in the Church, the gates of hell will not prevail against it. As the world was not fair to Jesus Christ, it will not be fair to His followers too. The path of a believer in this world is that of war but this war is fought not as the world does. Christ through death on the cross totally and irrevocably defeated and disarmed Satan both legally and dynamically. Now the Church has been given power and authority to carry the message of the cross to those who are perishing. God could put Satan completely away, but He has chosen to use him to give the Church crucial training in overcoming.[16] The Church has unlimited potential and God does not set arbitrary limits to the Church's use of divine resources. Paul Billheimer says; if the Church will not pray, God will not act. God will do nothing apart from His Church.

---

[16]   Paul, E. Billheimer, 1996, Destined for the Throne, Bloomington: Bethany House: page 91.

CHAPTER TWO

EXPOSING THE KINGDOM OF DARKNESS

The Fall of Lucifer

Everything in the kingdom of darkness begins with the rebellion and fall of Lucifer and consequently his defeat in the heavenly warfare. Satan's rebellion had to do with submission to God. Paul's statement in 1 Corinthians 11:10 that a woman ought to have a symbol of authority on her head because of the 'angels' suggests that one of the areas angels observe is that of submission to authority. Submission glorifies God while rebellion dishonors God. At the root of the angels' keen interest in what God is doing today is the rebellion and fall of Satan. As observers and part of the audience in heaven, all the angels were present when Lucifer, in his quest to be like the most high, sought to usurp God's sovereign rule (Isaiah 14:12-15). This was an offense to the glory of God. After Lucifer was fired (Ezekiel 28:11-19), war broke out in heaven and Lucifer was defeated and a third of the angelic hosts chose to follow Satan.[17] The lake of fire was prepared for him and his angels (Matthew 25:41) though he is not confined there now. His rebellion now has to do with God using the situation to demonstrate His glory, His grace and His justice.

The Devil's Names (2 Corinthians 11:14)

For us to deal with the enemy properly we must endeavor to know all his names and the spirit behind each name. A name generally shapes the destiny and character of the person.

The most common names of the devil are.

1. **Lucifer (Isaiah 14: 12 – 14).**
2. **Adversary (1 Pet 5: 8).**
3. **Devourer (1 Pet 5:9)**
4. **Serpent (Rev 12:9).**
5. **Prince of demons (Matt 12:24).**
6. **Devil (Rev 12:9; Job 1:6).**

---

[17]   Revelation 12:3 -4

7. **Accuser of brethren (Job 1: 6 – 11; Rev 12: 10).**
8. **Corrupter of minds (2 Cor 11: 3).**
9. **Father of lies (John 8: 44)**
10. **Tempter (Matt 4:3; 1Thessalonian 3: 5).**
11. **Satan (Rev 20: 3; 12:9 – 10).**
12. **Dragon (Rev 12:9).**
13. **'god' of this age (2 Cor 4:4).**
14. **Wicked one (Matt. 13:38).**
15. **Prince of the air (Eph 2:2).**
16. **King of devils (Matt. 12:24).**
17. **Angel of Abyss (Rev 9:11).**
18. **Evil one (Matt. 6:13).**
19. **King of Tyre (Ezek 28:1, 12).**
20. **Destroyer (Abbadon / Appolyon - Rev 9:11).**
21. **Son of the Dawn (Isaiah14: 12 – 14).**
22. **Belial (2 Cor 6:15).**
23. **Enemy (Matt. 13: 38).**
24. **Murderer (John 8: 44).**
25. **Thief (John 10: 12).**
26. **Deceiver (2 John vs. 7, Matt. 27: 63).**
27. **Prince of the World (John 12:31).**

There could be other names of the devil that are not indicated in the above list. The list is dealing with all the major ones. Looking at his names can actually reveal the works of the devil. We all know that the devil masquerades as an angel of light. He often times use **concealment and camouflage.** So it is important to know his names for ease confrontation. We can position ourselves better if we fully know his manes. The name of a person also reveals the characteristics of that person.

The Devil's Nature

The best way to deal with the enemy at any level is to find out what his nature is. Every move he makes on earth is something part of what he is already. The term 'devil' as used often of Satan, means slanderer, defamer, one who accuses falsely. As 'the slanderer' he is the one who defames the character of God and he does this mainly by accusing believers (Revelation 12:10). The book of Job gives a good illustration of his defaming accusations against believers and how, at the same time, he seeks to malign the character of God. In the first two chapters of Job, Satan's claim was that Job only worshipped God because of all God had given him; it was not because Job loved God for who He was or because God deserved to be worshipped as the Holy and Sovereign creator.

From the Bible's characterization of Satan as "adversary" (1 Peter 5:8) and the devil, and from his activities as seen in scripture, it seems logical that Satan may have argued that God was unloving and that His judgment of Satan and his angels to the lake of fire was very unfair and unjust. Shortly after the creation of Adam and Eve, the devil's attack on the character of God as unfair becomes immediately evident in the slanderous nature of his questions and statements to Eve in the temptation (Gen 3:1-5). He uses the same tactics even today.

Demonic Organization

The book of Revelation (chapters **12 – 22**) symbolically talks about the Harlot, the Beast, the false prophet and the dragon. Each of these is symbolic of something demonic or degree of evil. The '**dragon**' is the devil himself (Satan) who empowers every demon **(Rev 12: 9; 13: 2)** and goes about to deceive the whole world. The devil will also empower many people into the worship of the dragon. The great '**harlot**' **(Rev 17)** represents the false Church symbolizing demons of **immorality, idolatrous cities** and **rebellious humanity**. This also includes spiritual adultery (serving two masters or more), mixed beliefs and other blasphemous filthy activities. The first '**beast**' speaks of the manifestation of the Luciferian spirit as demons of social and secular power responsible for corrupt and devouring systems (systemic demons) of the kingdoms of the earth (Daniel 7:8). This includes today's social systems, political systems, and other world systems. This also speaks of human pride, authority, and the increase of fleshly desires on man for power and dominance. The next beast in (Revelation 19:20) is symbolized in the picture is the 'false **prophet.**' He represents a picture of demons of false religions and false worship, with deception as the common denominator and the controlling force. **(Rev16: 13)**.

The false prophet will cause many to go into false worship. Today the earthly forces, the heavenly forces, the ruling spirits or the principalities and authorities are networking and enforcing the application of the devil's plan on a global scale. Therefore, John encourages the believers in **Revelation 14: 12** to stay **patient and to endure and remain faithful to Jesus.** This is a great admonition to the Church. Faithfulness and endurance is what keeps us going.

The satanic hierarchy is as follows:

(a) **Satan (Lucifer)**
He is the devil; the fallen archangel **(Rev 12:7 – 9** - the old serpent) and Lucifer (brilliant star). The devil heads the kingdom of darkness as opposed to God who heads the Kingdom of light. The devil also known as 'the prince of this age' is the director and president of the satanic kingdom having with him all types of demons operating at different levels of authority. Every demon at all levels submits to him. He definitely seeks control and rulership on earth. The devil's expulsion from heaven to the earth means that, this world becomes his base of operations and that; his anger is vented towards the remaining inhabitants of the earth. So the devil himself marks the beginning of his hierarchy.

(b) **Principalities**
The word is derived from the word 'princes.' Since the devil himself is called the prince of the power of the air,[18] as we have already seen, the principalities or the chief rulers are ranked second in the Luciferian order. Principalities are principal rulers or commanders in the ranking of demons with high powers of governance. They rule over big areas of the

---

[18]   Ephesians 2:2

earth on behalf of Satan mostly at a national level. They are territorial in nature and in their operations **(Dan10: 12–15)**.The work of these principalities can bee seen in diversities of temperaments and cultures of the world. They occupy regions and areas of human existence carrying big influence upon the nation. The principalities cannot be exorcised. They can only be replaced.

(c) Powers

This category can be seen as demonic powers influencing areas of morality on people on a global scale. The word 'powers' indicate **'binding abilities'** or **dark angelic forces enforcing bondages** upon large groups of people on a global scale, for example, Johannes Fucius, the coordinator of Intercessors International remarks that, "alcoholism is one such global power enslaving millions of people all over the world, and binding them to the rule of Satan in their lives." It's not a sickness as many humanists claim but a demonic thing imposed upon people by the powers of Satan. This is indeed true of the spirits that are in this same context as alcoholism like smoking, homosexuality and lesbianism. These powers and other demonic forces are responsible for many people who are bound in yokes of slavery either physically or spiritually. Drug addiction is another example where these powers can also operate.

(c) Rulers

"Johannes Fucius sees a clear example of a 'demonic ruler' in 'Nazism' by Adolf Hitler whom he perceived to be nothing but a medium for a demonic ruler because he was deeply inspired by demonic spirits." He sees rulers to be something dealing with controlling spirits and powers enforcing corruption upon the people and upon other rulers who are masterminding the ideologies and philosophies behind it all. Some of these rulers are working to set up these heads of 'isms' and economic systems like Capitalism, Marxism, and Socialism etc.

The rulers rule by making decisions and policies that affect governments and ethnic groups. They rule on a national level with control over certain regional areas and cities. The devil many times uses people in positions of authority to besiege a city or a nation. These rulers always seek to control and manipulate other people. These rulers can be ancestral, oriental, secular, religious cults and so forth. The devil works through a lot human rulers and heads of state to cause oppression upon the people. The late Idi Amin of Uganda brought about the atrocities of humanity in the nation that saw many people losing their lives.

(d) Wicked forces in the heavenly places

Wicked spirits expresses the character and nature of demonic spirits operating in high places and in invisible realms. The old king James vision uses the words **'hosts of wickedness in high places**.' This indicates evil powers and Satan's department of religious and occult powers. High place is the Hebrew word **'bama'** which points to a shrine on hills o high places where altars were built. High places carry overtone of dominance and control. Biblically, high places were the major source of moral and religious collapse **(2 Kings 17:19)**, high places signify the practice of idolatry and witchcraft, and also places of worship of other gods. The term 'hosts of wickedness' indicates that we are dealing with those forces or armies in the satanic hierarchy which God considers to be the most wicked and probably the most dangerous. God says; 'you shall not have any other god beside me.' Anything which is mixture of God and other gods and occult practices results into false worship. The whole network of the New Age Movement is a clear indication of false worship. Hinduism in India and its spread to the rest of the world recognizes over 330 million gods existing in different names, shapes and sizes. Some cities have shrines and high places that most people have no idea of what they are. The arena of wicked forces in high places also includes demons assigned in the spiritual realm to hinder certain things from happening. Daniel 10:13 refers to the 'prince of the kingdom of Persia' opposing Michael. This was not the king of Persia but rather a fallen angel under Satan's control; he was a demon of high rank, assigned by chief of demons, Satan, to Persia as his special area of activity (cf. Rev 12:7).

The Consolation

The consolation from the Word of God is the fact that, no matter how complicated and diverse these demonic powers are, Jesus overcame them all. Paul says that 'He (Jesus) spoiled principalities and powers and made a show of them openly, triumphing over them all. The word 'spoil' means to strip the hide from an animal, to completely disarm the defeated foe, to damage or injure in such away as to make useless, to destroy.[19]

Demonology and Spiritual Warfare

One aspect of the ministry of Jesus when He was on earth was to cast out devils from people. The term 'demon' means, an evil attendant or spirit without a body. Demonology is **the doctrine of demons or fallen angles, their nature and what they do**. The whole purpose of demonology is deliverance. The doctrine of demons must be carefully studied so that Christians can best know how to deliver others from the power of demons. I have been involved in casting demons from people for over fifteen years and I have seen what demons can do to human life.

For those who deny the existence of evil spirits, take time to read the Bible and you will simply discover yourself that evil spirits are a reality. Demonology is a branch of angelology (**The study of angels both good and bad**), and angelology is a branch of Theology (**The study of God or the organized thinking about God**). So deliverance and demonology must not be separated from theology. Demonology and deliverance are all specific dimensions of spiritual warfare. "Deliverance means 'release and freedom from the powers of darkness or from the demonic spirits in the life of a person.'

Perhaps the challenge with most people is having the understanding of the terms demonization and demon possession. Some people have interpreted demonization as demon possession. Demonization is the experience of the characteristics of demons (demonized) manifesting in a life of a person. If a person has a demon of anger or gluttony, he or she is demonized but not really possessed. Demonization comes from the Greek verb (a verb is a doing word) *daimonizomai*, It means 'demonized' but in the sense of where one is doing the things that demons do.

---

[19]   Webster New World Dictionary

In the case of demon possession, one not only does what the demons do but he or she is taken as the devil's property and totally under the control of demons. Demon possession is where Satan and his demons inhibit a person to a greater or lesser extent. Demonization can happen to anyone, even a Christian but demon possession can happen only to those who are not born again. Demon possession is where Satan and his demons control the person as his own property. The difference between the two ideas 'demonization and demon possession' is the fact that, the former means 'you as a person you have some demons' and the latter means 'demons as spirits they have you. It is the battle between 'you having demons' and that of 'demons having you.' A true born again believer cannot be owned and led by demons because he/she is God's property. Those that are led by the Spirit of God are sons of God. The devil cannot lead a believer, he only tempts a believer. To the unbeliever, the devil cannot tempt him, he can only lead him. The devil cannot tempt his own, he just lead them whenever he wants and he tells them to do what hw wants them to do. Same with the Lord, He cannot tempt His own; He leads them to do what He wants them to do. Jesus in Matthew 4:1 was LED by the Holy Spirit to be TEMPTED by the devil. The leading was done by God, the tempting by the devil. This is a dominant theme in scripture (Amos 2:10; Psalm 23:2; Matthew 6:13; John 10:3; Romans 8:14, 2 Corinthians 2:14).

To expand further, demon possession involves six major steps: **regression, repression, suppression, depression, oppression and obsession**.

The steps in demon possession can be explained in the following ways:-

1. Regression:
This is the act of going backwards. It is the process of spiritual decline where a person is weakened by the enemy such that he can not make a positive decision. It is the degeneration and the falling off of person.

2. Repression:
This is a situation where a person is being held back by Satan from without little by little. It is the power of the enemy to dominate or subjugate an individual. At this stage, demons have set the platform for suppression and oppression but to a lesser degree.

3. Suppression:
This is the stage of restraint and demonic censorship where containment and control of demons gains momentum in one's life. Here Satan forcibly subdues, holds back, curtails or prohibits your spiritual growth and begins to control you and inhibiting you.

4. Depression:
This is the process of infusion of sadness, grief, despair, bitterness, disappointment, hopelessness and gloominess into one's life. These experiences eventually become demonic spirits. This is where now a person puts on the garments of heaviness due to failure of spiritual support systems.

5. Oppression:

This is the process of completely taking away someone's liberty bringing a person under coercion and demonic domination. There is a manifestation of feeling of heaviness physically and mentally. Demonic oppression is much more dangerous than human oppression. Political leaders can oppress people but it is easy to get them out of this kind of oppression than the demonic one.

6. Obsession:

This is fixation or compulsive preoccupation with a fixed idea or unwanted feeling or emotion, often to an unreasonable degree (E.g. lust). At this stage people are overtaken by the enemy and the spirit of resistance has been broken. The person is finally **possessed.** It means that, Satan inhibits and controls the person as his own property.

NOTE:

Some people who are under demon possession have entered into demonic or satanic covenants making the condition of the person even worse.

Characteristics of Demons

Demons throughout the Word of God have displayed their characteristics and a believer will do well to study these characteristics. Knowing the characteristics is not to be devil conscious but rather to master carefully the nature of the enemy so we can best deal with him.

*   Demons have intelligence **(Acts16: 16).**
*   Demons have doctrines **(1 John 4: 1).**
*   Demons have knowledge **(Matt 8: 29, Luke 4: 41).**
*   Demons have a will **(Luke 11: 24).**
*   Demons can respond back **(Acts 19: 14).**
*   Demons have memory **(Acts 19: 14).**
*   Demons move **(Luke 11:24; 8: 29).**
*   Demons examines **(Luke 11: 24).**
*   Demons speaks **(Acts19: 14, Luke 8:27 – 28).**
*   Demons controls **(Luke 9: 39).**
*   Demons have power **(Luke 8: 29, Mark 5:4, Matthew 8:28).**
*   Demons can reason **(Matt.8: 30 – 31).**
*   Demons have consciousness **(Mk 1:24, 5:7 – 9).**
*   Demons have a sense of future **(Matt. 8:29).**

Areas of demonic activities

Demons look for bodies where they can operate their program. They target key and strategic areas of human life. These could be looked at as activity centers of demons or spiritual battlegrounds where a believer has a war going on daily.

(1) **Emotions**- The devil appeals to our emotions through feelings of negative emotions such as bitterness, anger, rejection, hurt and so forth.

(2) **Mind** - Jesus was highly troubled in a place called Golgotha (place of the mind or skull). It is the reason why they crowned Him with thorns around the head to ensure that His mind was filled with doubt about the process. Satan appeals to our minds in several ways **(Gen 3: 1-3)**.

(3) **Tongue** – This untamed member of the body has power to create life and death at the same time. The devil works in this area through unclean speaking, lies, gossip, cursing, blaspheming and much more.

(4) **Sex** - This is an area where fornication, lesbianism, homosexuality, adultery, rape and marital unfaithfulness have become dangerous spirits of our society. Weapons of mass destruction are unleashed in this field.

(5) **Occult**-Demons work very much in the areas of witchcraft, charms, black magic, divination, necromancer, medium and sorcery. Some top officials, leaders and heads of states in some parts of the world rely heavily on magical powers or charms to sustain their thrones.

(6) **False religion** – One strong method demons prefer to work through is deception. The spirit of deception also manifests in religion. Religious devotions such as Hinduism, Mormonism, Shintoism, Sikhism, Hare Krishna, church of scientology, and cultism are among many distorted forms of worship.

Whatever the devil does, he plans it very well and he applies different strategies depending on the weaknesses of his opponents.

Satanic strategies always come through demonic activities. These activities are:

- To **entice** – temptation to do evil.
- To **torment** – to oppress with bitterness and unforgiveness.
- To **harass** – sexually, rape.
- To **compel** – to force to eat etc.
- To **defile** – bad pictures, pornography.
- To **deceive** – false prophet, false worship
- To **weaken** – infirmity, sickness, disease.
- To **control** – manipulate and besiege.
- To **blind** – prevent from truth, deception.
- To **enslave** – binding powers, ruling one's life.

Open Doors for Demons

Demons share domain with the world by finding rest in people or by residing in a place or region where they can achieve their mission. Demons always look for open doors. Demons can enter an individual by one or more of the following situations:

1. Personal involvement in occult practices like that of divination and witchcraft.
2. Ungodly relationships and unhealthy family soul ties.

3. Prenatal influence from mother to child.
4. Deliberate and willful submission to sin.
5. Inheritance, curses and iniquities.
6. Demonic objects and ornaments and other engraving.
7. Yoga, Voodoo, Satanism, Fighting.
8. Wrong religious covenants.

Dealing with spirits in altars and high places

Altars are mentioned in the Bible approximately 435 times of which 380 times the word is used in singular form and 55 times in plural form. The word altar is the Hebrew word 'Mizbeach.' It is a general word for 'altar' and it is translated as a 'place of sacrifice.' Another word is 'Madback' meaning, **'a sacrificial altar.'** The word **'ari – eyl'** referring to the **'temple altar in Ezekiel 43:15–16**). The Greek word is *'thusiasterion'* which means, a place of sacrifice." Thusiasterion comes from the word *'thusia'* meaning 'the act or the victim of sacrifice." Therefore the word altar simply means a place of sacrifice, a place of meeting God or a place of worship. These three - sacrifice, meeting God, and place of worship carries the whole idea of what altars should be. Hezekiah warned Judah and Jerusalem on the need for one altar of the worship of God **(2 Chronicles 32:12)**. So altars were structures upon which a religious sacrifice was offered. These altars vary in size, shape and purpose. Others may take form of a mound of earth, a heap of stones, one large slab of stone, wood or metal or even a trench dug into the ground like the Verdi altar of ancient India. An altar was considered a holy and revered object because of its deep religious meaning as a place hallowed by the divine presence. The altar allowed contact or communication with deities, other gods and spirits. Its power was so sacred and was well protected for commemoration and worship purposes.

Types of Altars

(1) **Godly altars** – for the worship of true God **(Gen 8:20)**
(2) **Demonic altars** – for the worship of Satan and operations of demonic activities **(2 kings 21:3 -9).**

Both the pagan or heathen and the Israelites built altars primarily for sacrifices. Roman and Greek cults made their altars in front of a sacred building and the altar became the focus and the center of their religious ceremony. The form and the position of an altar reflected its function. A raised altar was mainly used for sacrifices to the celestial deities in high places. Lower and underground altars served as receptacles for offerings to the gods of the earth or those gods of underworld. The pagans used their altars differently compared to the Israelites, and altogether they had different purposes.

In ancient Hebrew, altars were used both for animal sacrifice and for offerings of grain, wine and incense. In Christianity the altar held a far – religious meaning. It became a symbol of Christ and was marked with five symbolic wounds at its consecration. By the middle ages, the Christian altar had become a richly decorated throne on which they lay the consecrated bread and wine for the purpose of adoration and reverence. Islam is probably one of the religions that do not use the altars although their march to Mecca could be seen as a journey to a place of sacrifice. Mecca itself becomes an altar. The earliest and most evidenced of an altar dating from about 2000 BC is a named limestone structure excavated at the ancient Palestinian city of Megiddo.

Godly altars were erected for the following reasons...

- For refuge (**1 Kings 1:50 – 53; Ps 91: 9**)
- For access to God (**Gen 15:9 – 13; 35: 3 – 10**)
- For acceptance before God through the deeds (**Ex 24: 6 – 8; 1 Pet 1:18**)
- For witness (**Joshua 22:26**)
- For commemoration of what the lord has done to us. (**Exodus 17:15**)
- For burning incense – symbolic of prayer, intercession and worship (**Matt 5: 23; Rev 11:1; 8:5**).
- For thanksgiving (**Ex 17:15; 2 Chron 29: 27 – 30**).
- For protection (**2 Sam 24:18 – 25**).
- For ministry to the Lord (**Gen 12:7; 26:25**).
- Call on God (**Gen 13:4**).
- Authority increased (**Judges 6:32**).
- Meeting angels (**Gen13: 18**).
- Prophetic declarations (**1 Chron 22:1; King 8: 54 – 55**).
- Worship of God (**1 Kings 7: 48; 2 Chron 29: 27 – 8**).
- To receive blessings (**1 Kings 8: 54 – 55**).
- For attacking the enemy (**1 Kings 8: 80 - 32**).
- For prayer and supplication (**1 Kings 8: 54 – 55**).
- For the atonement of sin (**2 Chron 18 – 25**).

Idolatrous Altars and High places

God always destroys idolatrous, false and demonic altars (**Lam 2:7 – 8**) (**Judges 6:25**). The heathen nations led Israel into false worship that manifested in idol worship and establishment of demonic thrones and high places. These demonic altars were built in places of town, in mountains, in buildings (**2 Kings 16:10; 23:12, 15; Isa 27:9; Acts 17: 23**) and in many places. A high place is not the same as the altar, but it is a shrine on hills or mountains or high places where altars were built. High places have been known for dominance and control. They clearly included many pagan images such as standing stones, Asherah poles, sacred prostitution and other fertility rites. High places were the major source of moral and religious collapse (**2 Kings 17: 19**). Today many cities of the world do not realize how much impact the demonic altars are making to cities, nations or places. The devil has been using altars as one of the strategies of infiltrating communities with idol worship and other demonic activities. Most of our city altars today are control centers of most demonic events happening in our communities. The devil can make both personal altars and community altars.

Personal demonic altars involve specific individuals who have been agents of Satan given power to operate on a personal or individual level. Community altars are built for the whole community for the purpose of possessing the community. The other type of altar is the family altar **(Gen 35:1–6)** comprising of the members of one family. Building godly strong family altars is the key to city transformation. All demonic altars must be demolished to give way to godly altars. Today the focus of the altar is not on the size or shape but on purpose and function.

Demonic altars were erected for the following reasons:

- To initiate demonic influences over the area
- To dedicate the area to the enemy
- To sacrifice to spirits
- To worship Satan and his demons
- To hinder the flow of God's power
- To throw a demonic blanket over the people
- To embrace religious spirits
- To win favor and acceptance from their gods.
- To offer their own children to gods for food.
- To thank their gods.
- To appease their gods.

Most of the demonic altars act as demonic antennas or aerials attracting chaos and confusion in the area where they are erected. Some altars are in form of statutes, monuments, symbols, signs and objects.

Destroy altars by of the following methods:

- Remove the altars physically and pray.
- Renounce and resist the altars' effect on the area
- Release prayers of breakthrough in the area.
- Anoint affected areas consistently followed by warfare prayers and fasting.
- Disconnect by prayer the false gods, if any, associated to the altars in the region.
- Sing tehilah praises (High praises) to the Lord

Dealing with the Heavens

A person who wants to engage strategic spiritual warfare cannot help but study the heavens. There is probably more sophisticated war in the heavens than there is here on earth. Because of the strong presence of fallen angels that occupy the heavens, the level of spiritual warfare at that level is higher and tougher. God charges the angels with error (Job 4:18) is a sign of the level of contamination present in the heavens.

Isaiah 24: 21

> *"In that day the Lord will punish the powers in the heavens
> above and the kings on the earth below.*

Dealing with the heavens is an interesting part of spiritual warfare because we actually deal with the demons of the heavens or those atmospheres residing in the invisible domain. If the Church neglects what happens in the heavens, the end result will be dangerous. The Lord must rule in every sphere of life and in every area of creation.

When I talk of the heavens, I refer to mysteries, thrones, high places, high rulership, high cosmic powers, idols, things on earth and other powers in the heavenly realm. Demons are always drawn to places where they are invited. These places can be anywhere provided demons are comfortable with the situation. The demons in the heavens are difficult to determine unless information has been provided by God's angels. Daniel did not know that his answer was arrested by the evil prince of the Persian kingdom until he was told by the angel of the Lord.

In brief sentences, there are so far three atmospheric heavens according to **Gen 1:7 – 20** and later in scripture we have the fourth heaven of the highest where God resides (Matthew 6:9) or what Paul calls the third heaven.

Although Ephesians 2:10 talks about every knee bowing down in heaven, on earth and under earth; the term heaven can be used to describe all the levels mentioned.

The **1st Heavens** – the expanse of the sky or the heavens above with the greater light. This seems to be the heavens in Job 15:15 because in here we have the sun gods, the worship of the moon and many other spirits.

The **2nd Heavens** – this is a realm called 'the earth or the dry land' (Gen 1:9 – 10). Though earth is different from heaven, it is a heaven on its own.

The **3rd Heavens** – the heavens under-containing the accumulated waters or seas. This is the underworld. Some people reverse this order by starting from the under heaven.

The **4th Heaven** is the highest heaven where God dwelleth (Isaiah 66:1; Deut 26:15; 2Chron7:14). Elijah was taken to this heaven, Paul was caught up in this heaven and many lives also in current life have confessed having gone to heaven in sleep and so forth.

Demonic activities can operate in any of the above heavens except the heaven where God is. It is important that we deal with the heavenly realm because God made all the above **(Col 1:5; Ps 33:9)** for good purpose so that all creation can worship Him. The enemy should not be given room to operate in the heavens or do his business there. The heavens are to declare His glory. **Job 15:15** states that, "the heavens are not pure in His eyes." This is because the sin of mankind has gone further and higher than the heavens **(Ezra 9:6)**. If we look in The Bible, thrones were surrounded by magicians, sorcerers, astrologers, wise men and mediums **(Is 47:10 – 14; Dan 1:20; 2:27; 4:7)**. These were men who knew how to deal with the heavens and the waters. They always had connections with the stars, the moon and the sun. Examples of some of the thrones where the worship of the heavenly spirits is involved are as follows: -

(a) The throne of Egypt.

Egypt is one of the North African countries that have been known for the worshipping of the sun. Pharaoh was known to be the reincarnation of the sun god 'amunra.' Magicians, wise men and astrologers surrounded Pharaoh's throne. Moses encountered this throne to be one of the toughest experiences in his life at the time he and the Israelites were held captive. It took a series of plagues from the Lord for Pharaoh to release the Israelites **(Ex 8 12)**. This Pharaoh kind of power does not easily let go of God's people, and there is always a darkness that can be felt in such an environment. The gods of Egypt up to this day are quiet sophisticated and deeply rooted in idolatry. Pharaoh represents characteristics of the Luciferian nature in the way he deals with people. By studying Pharaoh, you will come to know the devil's nature in all aspects.

(b) Babylonian throne

Balaam came from Mesopotamia, a very close place to Babylon. Babylon was at this time the most important city in the whole region of Mesopotamia. The art of divination, astrology, astronomy, sorcery, accounting and private commercial law all stem from Babylon. Babylon was the potential area for demonic activities apart from its riches **(Dan 2: 27; 4: 7)**. This throne was possessive and manipulative. It is characterized by captivity, control and power, punishment and material objects. Babylonian throne represents super powers and highly developed human governmental systems. Babylon was a symbol of trade and global finance. God's purpose is to destroy the Babylonian systems.

Revelation 18:2-3

> *He cried with a mighty voice, saying, "Fallen, fallen is Babylon the great, and has become a habitation of demons, and a prison of every unclean spirit, and a prison of every unclean and hateful bird! For all the nations have drunk of the wine of the wrath of her sexual immorality, the kings of the earth committed sexual immorality with her, and the merchants of the earth grew rich from the abundance of her luxury."*

(c) Persian throne

In **Daniel 5,** God invisibly came to the party of king Belshazzar and wrote on the wall. The man's knees began to knock; the magicians and the wise men could not read anything. They all lost their reading powers – because God disconnected them and only Daniel was able to read. Christians need to learn this; God wants to render all demonic forces useless so that He can give us the place of victory. Esther and Mordecai worked out a prayer and fasting strategy to bring down Haman. Haman consulted the stars and it couldn't work because the power of prayer and fasting broke those lines **(Esther 4:3)**. The Lord wants the demonic thrones of our cities brought down by the power of prayer and spiritual warfare.

(d) New Testament Thrones

- **Simon of Samaria** in **(Acts 10; 19)** bewitched the whole entire region. He was a big sorcerer.

- **Paul met Elymas** the sorcerer, who hindered the spread of the Gospel. Paul called him 'a man of darkness' (**Acts 13: 8 – 12**) or the child of the devil (**NIV**). A sorcerer is one who tells lots or practices divination.
- Paul encountered the Queen of Heaven, the pagan fertile goddess in Ephesus. **Queen of heaven**, (Jeremiah 7:18; 44:17, 25) was the moon, worshipped by the Assyrians as the receptive power in nature. Ephesus was the center of the cult of Artemis. Artemis was a Greek virgin goddess of hunting. The Romans identified her as Diana. Artemis of Ephesus has been closely linked with the prominent goddesses of other demonic groups.

Artemis first appears in Greek literature as mistress and protectress of wildlife.[20] In Greece she was worshipped as the daughter of Zeus and Leto and the twin sister of Apollo. She was goddess of the moon and hunting. Tradition claims that her image fell there in Ephesus from the sky (etc. **Acts 19:35**), and is thought to rear to a meteorite."

The whole essence of the study on altars and high places is for the Church to know that God must be worshipped not the creation (**Rom 1:24**). The Church must cry for her cities because God has a purpose for each city. If we are to rule with Christ in the heavenly places, we must render total destruction of the evil powers in the heavenly realms.

One of the things to note about the heavens is that, there's much power in the heavens seeking government and rulership. Satan laid the foundations of enchantment, sorcery, star - gazing, astrology, necromancer and other things in Babylon. It began to spread to other parts of the world. Notice that one man who was important in the building of Babylon was Nimrod. He was a very heavy man in terms of sorcery and witchcraft. This is where the whole thing started. God would not allow such a thing to continue. So His move and purpose was to destroy Babylon (**Jeremiah 50:1 – 46; 51: 12**).

Acting out our strategies

We cannot remain silent after knowing all that is happening in the domain of darkness. For past years the Church has been slow and sometimes afraid of doing the right especially where application is concerned. The Church is a formidable force with enough power to overcome the powers of darkness. God has a plan for each city of the world. The worship of water spirits and the heavenly objects must come to an end. God has given us the creation and the heavens as our heritage. We are supposed to use these things (sun, moon, stars, water etc.) for good purpose. We must declare punishment on the heavens (**Isaiah 24:21– 23**) so that the heavens can be cleansed through *prayer and intercession* (**James 5:16b**). The Church must use the sun, the moon and the planets *to glorify* God. Every covenant that is made on earth, Satan has the records in the heavenly. Certain sicknesses and diseases are programmed according to the heavenly objects. The sun, the moon and the stars control astrology and stargazing. Most of today's witch doctors receive their enlightenment from the sun and the moon and of course from many other spirits.

---

[20]   **W.K. C. Guthrie, 1950, "The Greeks and their gods, , PP 99FF**

In Zulu language – **Njanga Onganga** means 'witch doctor.' It is actually the name that is connected to the moon. Most people go **mad** during the eclipse of the moon (the lunar eclipse). The word lunar means, 'the moon.' From here we have the word '**lunatic**,' which is translated as, **madness or insane.** The Moslems use the crescent moon to worship the moon god. Japan worships the sungoddess **'amaterato'** and other gods. Free masons have their signs connected with the worship of the sun. The constellations are highly used by a lot of people resulting into constant defilement of the heavenly places **(Job 15:15).** This is why the Lord will punish the powers in the heavens and the kings (rulers enforcing bondages on people) on earth (Isaiah 24:21). The problem is really universal and a big one. Only the Church has got the power to triumph over these forces. The ways and strategies of overcoming the enemy should be made known to every believer.

Cleansing of the Heavens.

To cleanse the heavens from all the forces operating in there, the Church must embrace the position Daniel took when the prince of Persia arrested his prayers. Daniel *prayed and fasted* with intensity to allow the angel to break through. By cleaning, it does not mean that the heavens will be free of demonic spirits but rather to fight the forces out of the way and to give way for God to intervene without any interference by the enemy. Cleansing of the heavens can be done at Church level or individual level. At Church level, cleansing the heavens requires the following preparatory foundations to be in place.

- **Unity in prayer and intercession (2 Chron 7: 14 – 15).**
- **Corporate repentance.**
- **Humbleness before God.**
- **Seeking God.**
- **Singing high (tehilah) praises.**
- **Practicing prophetic declarations and strategic intercession.**
- **Organized leadership.**
- **Engaging intense spiritual warfare.**
- **Practical evangelism.**
- **Holy Ghost inspired services.**
- **Declaring punishment to the powers in the atmosphere.**

A combination of all the above will make victory a possible thing. If we miss the application part and the strategy of getting into the enemy's territory, then we should not think of cheap victory. At individual level, one can cleanse the heavens by applying the following principles:

- **Strategic praying and fasting**
- **Positioning for breakthrough**
- **Prayer of punishing the powers in the heavens**
- **Resisting the frequencies of the enemy at work**
- **Praying warfare prayers**
- **Declaring spiritual authority to the principalities**

- **Persistence in breakthrough praying**
- **Releasing high praises in the atmosphere**
- **Waiting for the manifestation of the breakthrough**

Since the devil is the prince of the power of the air, it is important to defeat him also at the heavenly level of warfare. As a matter of fact, we rule with Christ in the heavenly places (Ephesians 2:6).

CHAPTER THREE
THE DEVILS MISSION

JOHN 10:10 (Living Bible)

> *"The thief's purpose is to <u>steal</u>, <u>kill</u> and <u>destroy</u>.*
> *My purpose is to give life in all its fullness."*

Understanding the devil's mission is always vital in spiritual warfare. It is the same mission that he has been working on from the time of his fall. His mission is to steal kill and destroy. He steals everything he can get from our lives because he is a thief.

Satan's Bid For World Control

Control is the primary purpose of the devil's mission. He is seeking dominion and authority over the nations of the world and to have total dominion over the human life. The book of Revelation **(18: 2– 3)** exposes the whole plan and activities of the devil's mission. He wants to control the trade of the whole world, the global finance, the material world, diplomacy and the human culture. The **Vision of the Enemy's Battle Plan** is disclosed as we look at the vision given to **Hollie Moody** on **25th April 2000. The vision goes as follows: -**

'LAUGHING AND TALKING WITH THE LORD'

As I was praying on April 25, 2000, I began to see in my mind a picture of the Lord. He was sitting on a rock and groups of people of all ages were gathered around Him. They all seemed to be laughing and talking together. I felt joy and peace and happiness as I viewed this scene. At times, the Lord would reach down and bring a child on to His lap. Or, He would reach out and a baby would be placed into His arms. He would then gaze down into the face of the baby and speak softly and tenderly to the baby. At other times, someone would draw close to His side, and He would place His arms around them, and draw them closer to Him.

'A WARRING ANGEL APPROACHES'

An angel approached the Lord. The crowd before the Lord parted to allow the angel to draw near to the Lord. A silence fell over the laughing, joyous crowd as the angel stopped before the Lord and began to speak.

From the way this angel was dressed, I sensed immediately that this was a warring angel. Being a warring angel and well were of the coming battle plan of the enemy; he spoke with a strong sense of urgency and even perplexity in his voice. He was very concerned.

"Why do the people sit here?" The angel said, meaning no disrespect. 'There is work to be done," the angel said to the Lord. "Why do the people only sit here idly? These are dangerous times. The people should be doing battle in prayer and in the spirit. Instead, they sit here at your feet, laughing. They are completely unaware of what is even now transpiring in the courts if hell."

With great concern in his voice, the angel asked, "Why are you allowing this?" (Before continuing the vision, as a side bar to that conversation, I had the impression the angel and the Lord had been in each other's presence numerous times and had many conversations with one another. What the angel said did not sound disrespectful or challenging at all. I could feel how he was feeling, and it was a genuine question in the midst of such perplexing opposition to come.

'SHOW THIS CHILD THE ENEMY'S PLAN'

The Lord gazed with love at the angel before Him, "Before I answer your questions," the Lord replied, "take this child of Mine and show her what is being planned by the enemy."

Both the angel and the Lord then turned their heads and stared at me. "This will be too much for her, "the angel protested.

"Take her, and show her," the Lord repeated. The angel bowed his head to the Lord, then turned towards me.

I began to go back nervously away as the angel approached me. "Where are you taking me?" I asked the angel. "To the enemy's camp," the angel replied.

"Go with," the Lord instructed me.

I felt very nervous and afraid, but allowed the angel to touch me. As soon as the angel touched me, we were in darkness. I felt fear engulf me.

'FEAR NOT'

"Fear not," the angel said to me, and instantly, the fear vanished. The darkness seemed to dissipate, and I discovered that the angel and I were in what appeared to be a great court. . A man was sitting on a large throne, and before him were gathered all types of creatures and men. (This "court" had the appearance of a cave. When I first viewed this scene, I felt stunned. I'm not sure why. It was like something "rebelled" in me at what I was seeing.)

"Who is that man on the throne?" I asked the angel. "And who are the creatures and men gathered before him?"

"That is the accuser of the brethren and his armies," the angel replied.

'WHERE SATAN RULES'

I then realized I was in the presence of Satan. (When the angel informed me that this man was Satan, the fact that he was sitting on a throne amazed me. Later, when I prayed about this aspect of the vision, I felt that Satan was trying to copy everything that was God's in heaven, for himself.)

Satan was speaking and I head him say, "This will be our strategy." He then got up from his throne and went to stand in front of a large map on the wall behind him.

As I stared at the map, I became aware that it was a map of the entire world. (It is very hard to describe this "map." The map wasn't actuary "pinned" or "hanging" on the wall, but it was in front of the wall. But, it was like I could see it from all angles. And also, I could see like "air waves," "Wind currents," the tides of the seas, etc. .I could also see the hemisphere around the world - moons, stars, planets, etc. I really have no words or way to correctly put down the appearance of this "map.")

'STRATEGIES AGAINST THE WORLD'

Satan began to divide the world into sections. Then, he called out some names. I saw the creatures and the men gathered before Satan's part, and very large and strong looking angelic beings approached Satan. (I saw four of these mighty looking angelic beings.) I could sense the power of these beings, and sensed the evil and wickedness of that power. A hush had fallen over the crowd.

"Who are these beings?" I whispered to the angel who I was with. The angel I was with seemed concerned. "They are Satan's princes." Satan began speaking again, and he was assigning sections of the world to each of these "princes."

"You will need your armies," Satan said to them. "Choose whoever you will. All is at your disposal."

'TO DECEIVE AND DESTROY MANKIND'

The large beings then began to pick and choose who would be in their particular army. (This was by no means "orderly." There was a great deal of arguing and bickering.) When they were finished, they all turned back to Satan and stared at him. "Each prince will teach you our strategy to deceive and to destroy and to slay mankind," Satan said. "Go with them."

'THE CLASSROOMS OF THE ENEMY'S SCHOOL'

The princes and their armies began to exit from the presence of Satan. The angel and I began to follow one of the groups. They went into what appeared to be a school room. The prince went to the front of the room and began to instruct his army on how to deceive, destroy and slay the people in their particular section of the world that had been allocated to them. The angel and I then went to each "classroom." The same plans and strategies were being "taught" in each "classroom." (By the "same" plans, I don't mean each class was teaching the exact same thing. What I mean, is that each class was very thorough in what it was teaching, and on how to apply what was being taught.)

In some of the classrooms, they were studying political leaders. Their families, homes and lifestyles were being closely scrutinized. I felt very frightened and helpless, very overwhelmed, as I saw and heard how very thorough these "lessons," for lack of a better word, were. Nothing was left to chance. Every area of these political leaders' lives was being dissected and investigated and studied. Demons were being assigned on how to "attack" and influence and "control" each of these political leaders, their families, and even their friends and co - workers. Nothing was left to chance. Nothing was overlooked. The books they read, the radio stations they listened to, everything, everything was being discussed. The enormity of all of this was absolutely mind boggling to me. This also occurred with the religious leaders.

'CLASSES IN RELIGION'

It was the "religion" classes that frightened and shocked me the most. In these classes, religions of the nations were being studied and discussed. Even new age and occult, Wicca and tarot were being discussed. Buddhism, Hinduism, etc., were being discussed. The Bibles and books and other writings for all of these religions were being read and studied.

Each denomination of Christianity was being studied. The Bible being studied was the major source of information for these "lessons". This was truly horrifying and shocking to me that demons were reading and studying the Bible. And, it was all for the intent to twist what was written, and to seek ways to misinterpret and misrepresent it to Christians. The demons were discussing ways to dilute the Gospel. They were "discussing ways to "incorporate" major beliefs from all the religions into one big acceptable "gospel of humankind."

'ORDERED TO INFILTRATE'

Some of the demons in these religion classes were ordered to "infiltrate" Churches, were being taken into actual Churches, and were watching how the people prayed, worshipped, sang, etc.

They were studying how messages were being delivered to the congregations in numerous Churches. They were studying the individuals who were used in the operation of the gifts of the Spirit. These individuals were followed around constantly by assigned demons, who watched and listened to everything these people said and did. The friends and family members of these individuals were also studied. The demons discussed ways to drive wedges between those people who were truly being used of God, and the people they went to Church with, and even how to cause these people's own pastors and spiritual leaders to lose faith and confidence in these people who were used in the gifts of the Spirit.

I felt so angry and frustrated and helpless as I saw and heard how this was to be accomplished, and how it had already been initiated in many, many congregations, and how it was largely succeeding.

'PRACTICING WORSHIP'

Many of these "religious" demons, for lack of a better word, were being taught how to sing in Churches, how to dance in the Spirit, how to pray and teach. I felt at times as if I were going to vomit as I witnessed many demons in these classrooms "practicing" how to worship the Lord, and how to be a Christian. Seeing a demon "dancing before the Lord" is so awful, and so sickening, that there are just no words to describe it adequately. Some more "major" demons could also work "signs, and wonders, and even miracles." Some of these demons were also being taught how to be "Christ." This was being done, by actually studying the scriptures. Seeing some of these demons acting and speaking like Christ shocked me speechless. Seeing them reading the Bible was like an abomination to me.

In some of these classes, even UFO's and aliens were being discussed, and how to deceive people through these phenomenon. There were classrooms where food and dress and slang words – yes, slang word! – were being studied and discussed. All of this was just so vast, it overwhelmed me.

Suddenly, the "classes" began to leave the rooms. The angel and I followed them. They congregated back in front of Satan.

'HOW WILL YOU DECEIVE MANKIND'

"Report," Satan said. "How will we deceive, destroy and slay mankind?"

One of the princes came forward and began to outline their plans and strategies to Satan. "The people want signs and wonders and miracles from their religious leaders," the prince said. "We know that our enemy will be, and has begun already, to grant this unto his children. We will slip in with a counterfeit move, and deceive many.

"We have taught our armies how to mimic worship, praise, and looking and acting like a true believer. We will give to our armies the ability to work signs, wonders and even miracles. But while all become focused upon these outward manifestations, others of us will begin behind the scenes to dilute the message of the Gospel. We will accomplish this partly through speaking to the people about God's 'true' nature.

The prince began to speak once again. "When the people have created their own version of God, then, we will give them OUR god." The crowd before Satan began to cheer wildly.

'BACK BEFORE THE LORD'

"We must depart!" the angel urged me. Suddenly, we were back before the Lord. He was still in the midst of His children; laughing with them, talking to them, touching them. A silence fell over the group once again as the angel I was with once more approached the Lord. The angel reported to the Lord all we had heard and seen in hell.

'WHY ARE YOU JUST SITTING HERE WITH THE PEOPLE, LORD?'

The angel was very concerned and distressed, asking, "Why are you just sitting here with the people? Why haven't they been sent to begin battle? How will they be able to discern this coming great deception if they aren't even aware that one is coming?"

The Lord became grave. His face as He looked at His children was alight with His great love for them. I noticed tears in His eyes. Then, He turned His head and looked at the angel speaking with Him.

'ONLY BY KNOWING THE TRUE WILL THEY KNOW THE FALSE'

"My children will know the false by knowing the true, "the Lord said. "The longer they stay in My presence, the more they will know My voice when they hear it. A voice of a stranger, they will not follow." "But the enemy has those who have been taught to speak just as you do," the angel protested. "They sound almost just like You. ""Almost," the Lord replied gently. "Almost they sound like Me. Only My sheep who have lingered long in My Presence will know the voice of their true shepherd. And this is why I spend so much time with My children. I spend as much time with them as they allow Me to. I know very well what the enemy is planning. My plans are plans of love and fellowship."

The angel and the Lord both fell silent as they gazed at the crowed before the Lord. "Love them well!" The angel replied.

'IN THE MIDST OF THE CREAT COMING BATTLE, I WILL MOVE, I WILL LESS.'

"Yes, a battle is coming, "the Lord sighed, and I saw tears in His eyes. "Great wickedness and persecution upon My children; My true children who know My voice. A time wickedness and persecution such as has never been seen or experienced. Yet in the midst of it all, I will move, I will bless, I will speak, I will love. I will win. There are those of My children who sense much of this. They are the ones who will never stop praying and interceding; not even in times of seeming peace." "What about me, Lord?" I asked.

'TELL THE PRAYER WARRIOURS TO STRENGTHEN THEMSELVES'

The angel and the Lord looked at me. "Pray," the Lord replied. "Tell the prayer warriors to strengthen themselves and their brothers and sisters in the times of peace. I will be pouring out of My Spirit upon all nations and peoples. It will spread to even the most unlikely of places – television, magazines, newspapers, radios, even the Internet. And it will be here that the battle will truly begin, and the deception begins."

'IT IS TIME'

The Lord stood up. "It is time?" the angel asked Him. "It is time," the Lord replied. Then, I was no longer with the Lord or the angel, but praying once again.

The End

This is without doubt a mind blowing, very moving, very touching and inspirational vision. A true and passionate intercessor cannot remain quiet after going through the vision of Moody. The question perhaps is, will the Church remain silent or do something about it? What brother Moody saw in his vision was just a glimpse of what goes on in the kingdom of darkness. Satanism is real.

The Church must indeed arise from slumber and move towards the battle lines boldly. We have read in the vision of Moody that the devil began to **divide the world, to deceive mankind, and to destroy human life**. The three words **divide, deceive and destroy** are of great importance in the devil's vocabulary. Today we see exactly the same happening in our time; divisions among organizations, deception among many people and massive destruction going on in many places of the world. The Lord is calling us to fight for our generations. We certainly must study the devil's character if we are to attack him properly.

Satan's Strategies in Warfare

It's important to look at some of the known strategies of the devil if we are to win the battle. Knowing his strategy helps the Church to fight with a focus. In order to recognize Satan and his works, we need to know his tactics and strategies so we can take our position of full power and authority over him. The Church must move from a defensive side to an offensive position.

The following are some of the strategies of Satan.

(1).Temptation (Gen 3: 1 – 6)
The scene of Satan and Eve in the garden gives us the first hand information on the dynamics around temptation. The devil made one move after another and he was very successful in getting man down. How this happened is very important and that's what every believer needs to know to avoid the temptation of the enemy. The devil's tactics in temptation is as follows:

1. He 'Misrepresents' and 'Misquotes' God's Word.

The devil's words were 'did really God say, you must not eat from any tree in the garden (Gen: 3:1).'If you compare Genesis 2:17 and Genesis 3:1, the devil twists and misreads the words in order to gain access and maximum advantage over Eve. It is his game of manipulation. If the devil can be successful in planting seeds of doubt in our hearts, he ends up taking control of our lives.

1. He 'Mixes' things up and 'Misleads' man.

Notice the response of the woman in Genesis 3:2 that she added extra lines 'you must not touch it.' In trying to defend her position based on what God had said, Eve it seems was very excited to challenge the devil and in the end, she started entertaining the enemy. The devil got her mixed up.

2. He 'Minimizes' the consequences of sin.

The devil said to the woman, 'you will surely not die.' This is the very thing he does today by sugar coating sin making it look appealing and less dangerous. He minimizes the consequences of our wrong actions and habits so we can keep doing them.

4. He 'Misreads' and 'Misplaces' the truth

The truth that God gave to Adam and Eve (Genesis 2:17) has been taken out of context by the devil. He misreads and misplaces the truth to create a longing for power and exaltation in Adam and Eve. The devil is simply telling Adam and Eve, this is your opportunity to become like God. The devil here is slowly misplacing man from where he is meant to be to where he is not supposed to be. He does the same thing in marriage, in business, in organizations and in families.

5. He 'Maximizes' the desire for things that lead to sin.

The devil's hit strategy is to maximize the desire to do wrong. He does this by appealing to our eyes. When Eve saw that the fruit was good for food and pleasing to the eye, and also desirable for wisdom, she took some and ate it (Genesis 3:6). The devil often times tempts people by way of sight. This is where the lust of the flesh takes super control over man.

6. He 'Messes' up the innocent.

Eve offers the portion of the fruit to her husband and he eats without questioning her or even reminding her of what the Lord has said to them. Obviously Adam loved Eve and it could be that he trusted her too much. Could it be that Adam did not see the nature and type of the fruit that was forbidden such that he ate the fruit thinking that it was from any of the tree that God permitted them? Certainly NOT! Adam knew the type of the tree and fruit; he just disobeyed God by letting the wife go ahead and share with him the fruit. If he didn't know, God would have vindicated him in the judgment. Adam neither picked the fruit nor was he deceived[21] by the serpent but he got punished too. Adam did not just eat the fruit; he was tempted by the tempter.

1Thessalonians 3:5

> *"For this reason, we could stand it no longer; I sent to find out about your faith. I was afraid that in some way the tempter might have tempted you and our efforts might have been useless."*

Temptation is the universal work of the devil and it always comes first on his program. The Lord Jesus was visited with temptation **(Matthew 4: 1 – 3)** by the tempter. The only exception is that, the devil cannot tempt those who belong to him; he can just lead them to do whatever he wants them to do since they are under him. The devil can only tempt believers because he knows that Christians are loyal to the Lord. His purpose for temptation is to get Christians out of the way of the Lord. Thank God that He will provide a way out for His obedient children. Evaluating further what happened in the garden, we see the lust of the eyes, the lust of the flesh and the pride of life being unleashed on Eve.

(2). Deception

Jesus after departing from the religious system, His disciples asked Him the questions about the sign of His coming and the close of the age (Matthew 24:1-4). He responded by saying that, 'watch out that no one deceives you.' He linked this deception to the religious system. Deception is one of the strongest points of the devil in unleashing his attacks on people. He deceives people by leading their minds astray. There many ways and areas where the devil can deceive people so easily. The Bible in 1Timothy 4:1 clearly says that, 'in later times some will abandon the faith and follow deceiving spirits and things taught by demons.' Most people who are in deception don't even realize that they are deceived.

John 8:44

> *"You belong to your father, the devil, and you carry out your father's desire. He was a murderer from the beginning, not holding to the truth, for there is no truth in him. When he lies, he speaks his native language, for he is a liar and the father of lies."*

---

[21]   1 Timothy 2:14

2 Corinthians 11:3

> *"But I am afraid that just as Eve was deceived by the serpent's cunning, your minds may somehow be led astray from your sincere and pure devotion to Christ."*

Deception is the native language of the devil. To every level of temptation there is a level of deception. Temptation is basically practical deception. The devil's plan of deception is to hinder as many people he can from coming to Christ. If there's anything that the devil is busy doing to accomplish his desires and goals, it's deception because he knows that his time is up. Deception is one of the greatest formulas of the devil in penetrating the nations with wickedness. This force of deception manifests and expresses itself in many ways and forms. Most of it has been false religion – e.g. Hinduism, Shintoism, New Age Movement, Mormonism, cults, Bahai. Other areas of deception are misrepresentation of Bible truth, falsehood and lies, distortion, and spiritual blindness. The devil always wants to sow seeds of lies in people **(Acts 5:3).**

(3). Disobedience and Unbelief

Hebrews 4: 6

> *"It still remains that some will enter the rest, and those who formerly had the gospel preached to them did not go in, because of their disobedience."*

The two words disobedience and unbelief cannot be separated because those who refuse to believe they in other ways disobey, and those who disobey end up living in unbelief. Disobedience and unbelief are relative terms. The devil's plan of disobedience is to hinder as many people as he can from coming to Christ. The end result of disobedience and unbelief is death or total rebellion. Total rebellion can be found both in the natural world and in the spiritual world **(Isaiah 1:19 – 20; James 2: 10 – 12)**. In the Christian world there is a steady increase of rebellion by some Christian leaders who have a problem of submission and humility. Instead of accepting correction or be humble in accepting advise, they insist on their way and in the end they rebel. The devil has been sowing seeds of disobedience through human ideologies and self-centered opinions that are not Bible based. God's idea is always better than man's ideas.

(4). Fear

Fear is another strong attack strategy of the enemy. This is mainly because fear attacks God's principle of faith. Faith and fear have got the same description. The difference is that fear attracts the negative; faith attracts the positive. If the devil can be successful in inducing fear in people, then he can easily attack them in all areas of their lives.

Gen 32: 7

> *"In great fear and distress Jacob divided the people who were with him into two groups, and the flocks and herds and camels as well. He thought, 'If Esau comes to attack one group, the group that is left may escape.'"*

The devil always smells fear and all his demons function on the basis of fear. One man of God said, '**FEAR** is when "False Evidence Appears Real." Probably what has killed many people today in most nations of the world is fear. This is because fear opposes God's principle of faith. In fear Jacob fled to Haran where he worked for twenty-one years. Jacob lived under the torment of fear. He was afraid of the unknown. Fear is a product of ignorance. Where fear is, the devil will be there. Fear can be the most dangerous stronghold because it seizes the whole entire person. Fear is a destructive spirit. It is the second and most common mental health problem. The Church must know that God's desire is for his people to walk in faith and love, and to have a sound mind **(2 Tim 1: 7). A man living under the yoke of fear will allow oppression and depression is his life.** Fear is what causes people to consult witch doctors over certain problems in their lives.

(5). Accusation and Slander

Rev 12:9 – 10

> *"The great dragon was hurled down - that ancient serpent called the devil, or Satan, who leads the whole world astray. He was hurled to the earth, and his angels with him. Then I heard a loud voice in heaven say: "Now have come the salvation and the power and the kingdom of our God, and the authority of his Christ. For the accuser of our brothers, who accuses them before our God day and night has been hurled?"*

The devil seeks to oppose and accuse saints before God. He is a slanderer. He wants to make Christians feel guilty and condemned before God. He will always find a platform where he accuses us of something we have not done. The devil does all this to gain access to the human mind **(Acts 5:3, 1 Pet 1:13; 2 Cor 12: 9 – 10, Genesis 3: 1 – 5).**

The mind is today recognized as the most sensitive and dangerous battleground. The Christian walk depends on our minds. The untrained mind will be the field for demonic activities. The human mind has been the target area of the devil. To win a person, Satan has to appeal first to the mind of the person and once he succeeds in getting the mind, he can now get the whole person. The mind is one area where we are all required to overcome the devil. Our minds should therefore be renewed by the Word of God everyday **(Rom 12:2).**

Three Aspects of Devil's Mission

John 10: 10 – (AMP)

> *"The thief comes only in order to steal, kill and destroy. I came that they may have and enjoy life, and have it in abundance to the full, till it over flows."*

The key words in the above passage are: **Steal, Kill and Destroy**. The devil has a lot of doors to accomplish each task. Some of the doorways are....

Inheritance, blood contracts and sacrifices, drugs witchcraft, kung-fu and karate, cannibalism, sex, incest, illness and disease, rock music, hypnosis, occult and horror movies, rebellion, drunkenness, animal and human sacrifices, murder, yoga and Satanism, idols, martial arts divination, pornography, false religions, racism, child abuse, alcoholism, smoking, etc.

All these have been areas where people have been either killed or destroyed and have been robbed of their true identity. A brief understanding of his mission is important in warfare.

(1) Stealing

The devil seeks to steal people's identity. He comes to steal health, joy, finances, peace and possessions. Many people have been robbed of their true identity and self-image. Above all, the devil wants to steal 'life' which God gave to mankind to enjoy when He created man. Many people are short of real life because they are under the heavy blanket of Satan.

(2). Killing

Today the rate of murder and killings all over the world is highly frightening. The situation is universal. The devil is busy strategizing on how to kill life. We have more premature deaths today than before. Anything that the devil puts his hand to – there's always a negative effect to it. Today HIV-AIDS is a huge threat to human security. Demons all over the world are seeking whom to devour. It seems at the moment that the world's death rate is higher than its birth rate. Jesus came to give abundant life. Though there are images of fighting and death in the Bible, the Bible is a book of life throughout.

(3) Destroying

The devil always seeks to destroy life, nations, people groups, Churches, religion, schools and culture. There's more of distorted religion today than of true religion. The devil's work of destruction has no respect for age, religion, family size, nation or color. That's the nature behind his names. He feeds on destruction. He has always attempted to destroy human life all over. Corruption, moral degradation, worship of idols, disease and sickness, astrology and human sacrifice are all various levels of destruction. All his strategies and plans points to one word - **destroy**. Thus if we are to stop him, we should destroy all his works **(1 John 3: 8b)**.

CHAPTER FOUR

PREPARING FOR SPIRITUAL WARFARE

The Battle Ground and the Battle Lines

Everything in life works well with preparation. It is the responsibility of those engaging in warfare to know exactly how to assess the battle ground and how to draw the battle lines. Gethsemane experience was the battle ground for Jesus and He drew different battle lines depending on the type of situation He encountered. His victory depended more on His stand rather than His fight.

Ephesians 6: 13 (Amp)

> *"Therefore put on God's complete armor, that you may be able to*
> *resist and stand your ground on the evil day (of danger), and, having*
> *done all (the crisis demands), to stand firmly in your place."*

The Greek word for 'stand' means, **"hold your ground or be firm as you fight against your enemy."** 'Battle-front' is a concept of strength and determination to face the enemy head on.' There is no need for fear of facing the enemy because the battle belongs to the Lord. To cross the battle lines is to enter boldly into the territory of the enemy and gain the victory over the enemy.

1 Samuel 17:32

> *"David said to Saul, "let no one lose heart on account of this*
> *Philistine; your servant will go and fight him."*

David faced the giant Goliath with boldness and determination to win. David knew that the battle was the Lord's. In verse **48 - "As the Philistine moved closer to attack him, David ran quickly toward the battle line to meet him."** David for sure is an example of a front - liner. The Church must get quickly to the front and fight.

Watchman Nee says; "we have our position with the Lord in the heavenly, and we are learning how to walk with him before the world; but how are we to acquit ourselves in the presence of the adversary – his adversary and ours? The Church is called to displace Satan from his present realm and to make Christ head over all."

The term 'stand' implies that the ground disputed by the enemy is really His (God's), and therefore ours. Defensive warfare always seeks to maintain the ground and keep it, where as in offensive warfare, a person has no ground but he is fighting in order to get the ground and advance further. Offensive warfare goes forth to attack, and to possess. Our Lord Jesus was offensive in His approach of dealing with enemy.

As we prepare for war, we need to know the battlefield and the battle lines. In Christ we do not fight in order to win or for victory; we fight from a position of victory **(Rom 8: 37)** because in Christ we have already won the battle. In Christ we are more than conquerors.

So the battle-front simply means, facing the enemy without fear and go right in front where the battle is and draw the lines of victory because we already have the victory. The following scripture below is another good example of breakthrough spiritual warfare.

2 Sam 23: 16

> *"So the three mighty men broke through the philistine lines, drew water
> from the well near the gate of Bethlehem and carried it back to David. But
> he refused to drink it; instead, he poured it out before the Lord."*

Out of a large number of Israelites who needed to face the lines of the Philistines, only three made it, the rest fled. If the Church today starts living in fear, she will even lose the victory she already has. We must do everything it takes to be in front and declare our victory in the territory of the enemy. We have His power, His dominion, His strength, His armor, His blood, His Spirit and His Word. The gates of hell should not prevail. Paul saw the power of God in his ministry such that, those who withstood the Gospel asserting themselves against Paul and Peter were led away blind.

If we are to prepare for spiritual war, we must really understand that we must be in front not at the back. Esther had battle lines with Haman **(Esther 4:15 – 16)**, she said: "And if I perish, I perish." Warfare is a risk taking business. Very few of us can make such a statement. To make matters worse, she went on to invite Haman the murderer to sit at the same banquet table with **(Esther 5:4)**. This is true of David when he said; 'The Lord prepares a table for me in presence of my enemies **(Psalm 23:5).'** **A feast verses a fight** is what is implied here. **'God never omits our enemies on His program of dealing with us.'**

Jesus began His ministry with a combination of **fasting and fighting (Matt 4: 1- 5)**. The last part of **Rev 12: 11** is another interesting and important part for many Christians to look at. It says, **"They overcame him (the devil)……….. because they did not love their lives so much as to shrink from death."** In other words they were prepared to die for the cause of Christ. They were not afraid of death. It talks about life-riskers not jockey - Jam Christians. Life riskers are men and women who are prepared to say: **"If I perish I perish."** Pause for a moment and think about yourself in the light of what I have just said in his passage. I believe one of the challenges that will go through your mind is; can I do it. Lord?

My answer is yes! You can do it, just put aside yourself and let God do it through you. Set aside every natural limitation. The creation for sure waits for the true sons of God to be revealed **(Rom 8:19)**. David says: **"My boundary lines have fallen for me in pleasant places," (Ps 16:5)**. So do not forget to claim your boundaries. In spiritual warfare the more we step forward the more we get stronger; the more we step backward the more we live in fear.

Weapons of Spiritual Warfare

2 Corinthians 10:4

> *"The weapons we fight with are not the weapons of the world. On the contrary, they have divine power to demolish strongholds."*

In spiritual warfare or any other type of war, weapons are an integral part. The Word of God urges us to put on the whole or complete armor of God and embrace all other weapons of war. We can only be strong in the Lord and in the power of His mighty **(Eph 6:10)**. God has given us weapons that position us above defeat. Most of the weapons can be used as offensive weapons.

Victory does not lie in weapons; it lies in the right use of the weapons.

The weapons we have as believers are as follows:

(a) Faith (Hebrews 11:6)

The very first powerful weapon in spiritual warfare is faith. Our fight as believers is that of faith.[22] We face giants in faith and we obtain victory by faith. Without faith it is impossible for believers to please God.

Mary Garrison defines faith as **"strict adherence to the Word of God, fidelity, loyalty, care observance, exact, accurate and recognition of spiritual realities and principles as supreme."**

All spiritual warfare starts from here. No one can please the Lord in warfare without faith. A man of faith can overcome any kind of obstacle in life. The devil knows that faith overcomes and thus he wants to keep many people in fear so he can operate freely. A good fight must be fought in faith. The faith chapter of the Bible **(Hebrew 11:33 – 35)** explains the miracles and the power of faith.

---

[22]   1 Timothy 6:12

1. Faith subdues kingdoms.
2. Faith can stop and shut the mouths of lions (Stop the lies of the devil and take dominion over the demons)
3. Faith can quench the fury of the flames (the violence of the fire and the devil's fire)
4. Faith knows how to escape the edge of the sword.
5. Faith can make the weak strong – (faith is power and energy).
6. Faith can rout all foreign enemies (Turn to flight the armies of the aliens)
7. Faith can conquer death – (overcoming faith.
8. Faith obtains God's promises.

Daniel and David are good examples of men of faith who all waged war believing that God was doing what He said He would do. They faced their giants in the spirit of faith and in the name of the Lord.

(b). The Name of Jesus

The name of Jesus is not only for our salvation but also for us to be able to appropriate the victory He has given us. It is through Him that we have power to do all things. The devil cannot stand the name of Jesus.

Luke 10:17

> *"The seventy two returned with joy and said, "Lord, even the demons submit to us in your name."*

Victory begins with the name of Jesus on our lips. The name Jesus is a powerful tool in spiritual warfare and deliverance. The name of Jesus has such great power to disorganize and destroy the whole entire kingdom of darkness. All other weapons cannot fully function without the name of Jesus. All demons are fully aware of this fact.

(c). The Word of God

Jesus conquered Satan by the power of the Word. He clearly indicated to the devil that man shall not live by bread alone but by every word that proceeds from the mouth of God.

Ephesians 6:17

> *"Take the helmet of salvation and the sword of the Spirit which is the Word of God."*

The Word of God puts Satan to flight because he can't stand it. The Word of God is the sword of the Spirit sharper than any double-edged sword. This means, there's no area or region too hard for the Word of God to penetrate. The Word of God has got power to melt and destroy all the plans of the devil **(Jeremiah 23:29; Psalm 149:6)**. The Word of God is both a defensive and offensive weapon. It defends us and it defeats the enemy. The power of God's Word is indeed power to work all that God wants to do. We too can overcome by His Word **(Rev 12:11)**. Jesus overcame the devil through the Word **(Matt 4:1-4).**

(d) The Blood of Jesus

The blood of Jesus is a powerful weapon but it is how we understand and use it that determines its application. It was obviously shed once but its efficacy still applies. We have been justified by His blood (Romans 5:9).

Revelation 12:11

> *"They overcame him by the blood of the lamb and by the word of their testimony; they did not love their lives of much as to shrink from death."*

Demons are always under torture whenever the blood of Jesus is mentioned. His blood was shed to give us total victory over the devil.

(e) The Holy Spirit

The Hebrew word for 'spirit' is *ruach*. It primarily means 'to breathe out through the nose with violence. It is an onomatopoetic word similar to *puach* and *naphach*, both of which mean 'to breathe out through the mouth with a certain amount of violence or even 'to blow out.' *Ruach* carries the idea of wind and power. Isaiah (11:4) captures this thought when he says; 'the Lord will slay the wicked with the breath (*ruach*) of His lips.' The word *ruach* stands for strong, hard, violent breathing, as against *neshamah*, which means ordinary, quiet breathing. *Ruach* is not flesh, but is of God and is the agent of God. The phrase *ruach-adonai* stands for the special power by which God inspires the individual man, enabling to do the will of God, thus to do those things which in his own strength he is wholly unable to do. Prophets prophesied by *ruach adonai*. Jesus conquered the devil in the power of the Holy Spirit. He healed and touched the oppressed through the anointing of the Holy Spirit. We too in spiritual warfare can use the Holy Spirit to stop all the advances of the enemy.

Zechariah 4:6-7

> *"So he said to me, "This is the word of the Lord to Zerubbabel; "not by might nor by power, but by My Spirit," Says the Lord almighty."*

> *verse 7 - "what are you, O mighty mountain? Before Zerubbabel you will become level ground. Then he will bring out the capstones to shouts of 'God bless it! God bless it!"*

It is the spirit in which we do things that determines the things we get in life.

Deliverance and spiritual warfare without the Spirit of God is not possible. The Holy Spirit is the anointing that breaks the devil's yoke **(Isaah10: 27)**. Demons of all sizes cannot stand the power of the Holy Ghost. Jesus came in the anointing of the Holy Spirit and the devil could not stand His power. The Holy Spirit knows how to deal with every level of darkness just as it was in the beginning **(Luke 4:18; Acts 10:38; Gen 1:1-3)**. We should not make any attempt to do spiritual warfare without the Spirit of God.

(f) Our God given authority

Luke10: 19

> *"I have given you authority to trample on snakes and scorpions and to overcome all the power of the enemy; nothing will harm you."*

Though God has given us authority over the devil, we can only expect to see spiritual breakthrough to the degree we receive and apply the God given authority in prayer, spiritual warfare, preaching and in other areas of ministry. We cannot fight the devil without using the God given authority **(Luke 10: 19).** Authority means, **power, capacity, control, competence, rule, legality and force**. The Kingdom of God needs forceful men **(Matt 11:12)** who carry authority and influence. Much of this authority comes from the Word of God. Only when we obey the Lord can we flow in this authority. There's enough grace at the cross for all of us to maximize this authority.

(h) Our Obedience to God

My personal experience coupled with research in spiritual warfare has taught me that, obedience makes warfare easier and it is perhaps the most powerful weapon in spiritual warfare. All other weapons will fail to function if obedience is not in place.

2 Corinthians 10:5-6

> *"We demolish arguments and every pretension that sets itself up against the knowledge of God, and we take captive every thought to make it obedient to Christ. And we will be ready to punish every act of disobedience, once your obedience is complete."*

Obedience is a primary and key weapon in spiritual warfare. Jesus in His prayers to the Father demonstrated a high degree of obedience and His prayers were heard because of the same (Hebrews 5:7-8). It is when we are obedient to God that we become friends with Him.

Psalm 81: 13 – 14 says,

> *"If my people would but listen to me (obey me), if Israel would follow (obey) my ways, how quickly would I subdue their enemies and turn my hand against their foes!"*

Obeying God is the quickest and surest way of defeating the enemy. We cannot declare punishment on the forces of darkness until we first of all show our complete obedience to Christ. The devil and his demons cannot be underestimated. He (God) who is in us is greater than the one (devil) who is the world.

Personnel Profile for Spiritual Warfare

Though there is a general call for all Christians and believers to pray, intercession and spiritual warfare requires serious and mature Christians. Spiritual warfare is for those believers who are forceful, vigilant and well prepared. Joshua chose best fighting men. David had the three mighty men who broke through the lines of the Philistines. It is imperative when going to war that, an army should carry experienced and prepared soldiers.

Luke 14:31

> *"Or suppose a king is about to go to war against another king. Will he not first sit down and consider whether he is able with ten thousand men to oppose the one coming against him with twenty thousand."*

Joshua 10: 7

> *"So Joshua marched up from Gilgal with his entire army, including* <u>all the best fighting men</u>*."*

Matt 11:12

> *"From the days of John the Baptist until now, the kingdom of heaven has been forcefully advancing, and* <u>forceful men</u> *lay hold of it."*

No army today in the world can go to war without considering the type of personnel to be involved in war. This happened to Gideon when the Lord asked him to cut down the number of his army to only a minority of quality personnel **(Judges 7:1-8)**. Those that are newly recruited in the army cannot go to war due to inexperience and inability to handle the weapons and the opponent effectively. To send untrained men for war is a commitment or a deliberate plan to produce victims and casualties. Untrained personnel will always graduate from battle as casualties. Today the world has more victims than victors, more casualties that conquerors. We cannot afford a spiritual warfare that takes place in a complete vacuum. The Church must realize that it takes men and women trained body, soul and spirit to produce best results in ministry. If we just send people to war because there's a need to fight, we are playing with fire. Apostle Peter urges the Church to alert and vigilant **(I Peter 5: 8)** because the devil is busy looking for weak Christians. Spiritual warfare is a do or die situation.

It is really dangerous to carry inexperienced solders to war (Judges **3: 1 – 20)**.

Verse 1- "These are the nations the Lord left to test all those Israelites who had not experienced any of the wars in Canaan (he did this only to teach warfare to the descendants of the Israelites who had not had previous battle experience)."

Not everyone can do constructive spiritual warfare. The Church needs forceful and capable men to do the work of Spiritual Warfare. David in **Psalm 18:34** made a very important statement "…. He trains my hands for battle; my arms can bend a bow of bronze." It takes a trained **spirit, soul** and **body** to make a difference in spiritual warfare.

Spiritual warfare is one area of ministry where only the serious people will realize the results because it's a matter of death or life. Below are some of the characteristics of right personnel in spiritual warfare….

(1) **C**ommitted to the Lordship of Jesus Christ.

(2) A spiritually balanced life (Rom 8:14).

(3) The fear of the Lord. The fear of God kills all other fears (Numb 14:24).

(4) Passion for prayer; not necessarily an intercessor (Mark 9: 29, Matt 17: 21).

(5) Established in God's Word and be prepared to use the Word of God in all situations (Ephesians 6:17; Rev 12:11).

(6) Disciplined and determined to serve the purposes of God (Num 13:30, Dan 6:1).

(7) Sound relationships with the Lord, the family, and friends.

(8) Purity and righteousness: Sin always hinders people from receiving a breakthrough. A sinner for sure cannot overcome the devil (Acts 19: 14 - 19; Eph 4: 27).

(9) Walking in faith (Heb 11:6).

The devil knows how to capitalize on our weaknesses. So it's really of great importance to use right people in spiritual warfare situations. The Lord made Jeremiah a fortified city (a strong man) and an iron pillar (a solid soldier), and a bronze wall (An attacking warrior) and then released him to fight **(Jer 1:17-19)**. He was well prepared by the Lord.

Locating the Enemy

It is always dangerous to fight with the enemy you do not know. We must first possess the knowledge of our enemy before engaging him in war. We need to locate the enemy and assess his strength and then bind him and claim our territory. The challenge of spiritual warfare is always in identifying the strongman **(Luke 11:21-22)**. We must bind the enemy first and then take all the goods that belong to us. If we take a look at the early Church, we see that the apostles were able to locate their enemy.

What characterized the early Church spiritual warfare dynamics is their knowledge of the enemy. The apostles fought spiritual warfare effectively because...

- **They recognized the existence of evil spirits**
- **They knew that evil spirits deceived men.**
- **They understood the devil's purpose**
- **They knew the reality of spiritual battles**
- **They recognized their enemies**
- **They never underrated the enemy**
- **They located their enemy**
- **They recognized the characteristics of demons**
- **They knew the schemes of the devil very well**

We cannot fight effectively without locating the enemy and his strength. The following brief questions are some examples of how to locate the enemy at work in our area.

- What kind of enemy are we dealing with in our area, society or community? Is it fear, sexual immorality, witchcraft etc.
- What is the enemy doing to our people in the community or nation?

- What are the common demonic activities taking place in our city or town area.
- Are there any certain natural sites or buildings that are widely believed to be haunted, dedicated to Satan or demonized?
- What gods are worshipped in non-Christian circles?
- Are pagan rituals, ceremonial and traditional dances been performed in our region?
- How are people responding to the Lord in the region? Are the Christian Churches active or inactive in our area?

There are many more questions that can be asked to assess the enemy at work. In military, when it's time for war, the commanding officer or the general in charge of the mission informs all the troops of the type and nature of the enemy. He thereafter advises the army about which direction should the army take. It is not everyone whom the soldiers meet becomes an enemy. Only those who are defined and described within the context of the war should be considered enemies. If we ignore the enemy and his characteristics, we will end up limiting our chances of defeating him. Jesus after crossing the lake into the region of Gerasenes met a demon possessed man begging Him not to torture the spirits. Jesus asked possessed man; "what is your name?"(Luke 8:30). The man's name was legion. Legion implies a maximum of 6000 demons. Jesus asked the question because He wanted to know what kind of enemy He was dealing with. Spiritual warfare is best fought after the enemy has been located.

To locate the enemy therefore is to.

- **To assess the strength of the enemy**
- **To appraise the battle field**
- **To know the form of the enemy**
- **To know him fully as he is not as he appears**
- **To know what the enemy represents**
- **To discover our enemies**
- **To know the devil's position**
- **To bring him on the surface**
- **To know is characteristics**
- **To know is nature.**
- **To have a full picture of him**
- **To know what he likes**
- **To know his moves**
- **To know whom he uses**

The point is, understanding the activities of enemy makes it will be easier for the Church to do effective spiritual warfare.

Warfare Language and Terms

One of the most frustrating times I have had in my practical involvement in spiritual warfare is to pray with people who do not rightly use and understand the terms to use in spiritual warfare. A good mixture of spiritual words is an integral part of spiritual warfare. Wrong use of terms will not lead to effective warfare. Spiritual language must be used in agreement with the context and the purpose that is attached to the language. We are urged in the Word of God to combine spiritual thoughts and truths with spiritual words (1 Corinthians 2:13). Many people don't realize how important the use of words is in prayer. The concept of telling people that God understands when we should do the right thing is a big distortion of spiritual realities. Its quiet true that God knows what is in our heart (both good and bad), but it is very important to use the required and accurate language in each case or situation. Spiritual thoughts give birth to spiritual words.

Praying and engaging the enemy through prayer requires......

- **Clarity**
- **Simplicity of heart and altitude.**
- **The use of correct words**
- **Aptly words**
- **Straightforward words**
- **Biblical words**
- **Well-known words**
- **Specific words to specific situations**
- **Contextual words**
- **Consistent terms**
- **Removal of unnecessary repetitions**
- **Applicable words**

The most commonly used words in spiritual warfare are, bind, loose, destroy, frustrate, break, demolish, paralyze cast out, uproot, rebuke, stand against, extinguish thwart, confuse, come against, resist, possess, overcome, cut-off, release, curse, take authority, crush, disarm, dismantle, claim.

One thing to note is that the above words cannot apply in every spiritual warfare situation. For example it's wrong to say, 'we dismantle or break Satan,' because the devil as a creature or being is only one, and if we dismantle him we don't expect him to function any more in the whole world. His time of destruction is in the future not now. Only the God of peace will crush and finish him off at the close of the age when his time is finally up. Meanwhile, the devil is the god of this age and the prince of the power of the air. So there's no need for us to break the devil today when we know he will certainly be there the following day. But we can resist him **(James 4:7)** and destroy his works and those things under his operations. We can break the yoke of slavery to sin from people, we can break the chains of Nazism, we can cast out demons, and we can destroy demonic altars. All this we can do without fail but not destroying the devil.

The devil knows that where there's ignorance, he can easily succeed. I challenge every Christian to take note of terms and words whenever praying especially in the context of spiritual warfare. Jesus did not come to destroy the devil; He came to destroy the **works of the enemy (1John 3:8b)** which means, **to melt, to dissolve, to cut-off or put-off, to**

loosen and to destroy. So it's important for the Church to understand fully the importance of language in spiritual warfare. A play of words doesn't help because there's no confrontation with the exact forces of darkness. Spiritual warfare needs men and women with the language of the Bible and well prepared with proper terms.

The courage to fight

After all has been said and done, the courage to fight is what completes the preparation as far as spiritual warfare is concerned. Many people do enjoy preparing for war but they lack the courage to show up for the fight. A place of courage is what defines those who are truly warriors and those who are not.

Deuteronomy 31: 6

> *"Be strong and courageous. Do not be afraid or terrified because of them, for the Lord your God goes with you; he will never leave you nor forsake you."*

Jeremiah 1:17

> *"Get yourself ready! Stand up and say to them whatever I command you. Do not be terrified by them, or I will terrify you before them."*

In the second scripture, God's word to Jeremiah was, **"Be ready, fear not or take courage and face your enemy."**

No one should attempt to go to war without being ready and courageous enough to face the enemy. This is because people who are well prepared, ready and courageous have what it takes to face the enemy. The Church of Jesus Christ is a courageous Church. A place of courage is a place of confidence and hope which is mainly characterized by the desire to conquer the enemy and the power to possess. If we closely take a look at **Numbers 13:30,** Joshua and Caleb proved to be men of courage and confidence. God was prepared to take the two into the Promised Land because of their courage.

The Courage to fight is the Foundation of Christian Victory

There's no fear in the courageous zone. Courage is the only last thing that an army needs after acquiring all primary requirements. In the absence of courage there's disappointment, fear, giving up and loss. God is looking for a courageous team of believers well determined to carry out God's purposes on earth.

The following below are some of the main ingredients of courage.

- **Faith** - Total trust and dependence on God
- **Confidence** – The inner drive, that hope, trust and belief in God that He will do it irrespective of the situation or circumstances around.
- **Hope and Assurance** – Total conviction that God's promises will not fail.

- **Zeal** - This is stamina and enthusiasm to do something with a purpose. Zeal cannot be separated from courage.
- **Boldness** - We need not to fear the devil and his demons. The righteous are as bold as a lion. We must face any situation in whatever state it may be. The early Church is a good example of a people of boldness. There's no courage that does not include the aspect of boldness. Every courageous Christian is a bold believer.

CHAPTER FIVE

DIMENSIONS OF SPIRITUAL WARFARE

Practical Spiritual Mapping

The principles of spiritual mapping are almost the same throughout the world, but the methods are not the same because it varies from one place to another. Some parts of the notes have been taken from the spiritual mapping Field Guide by George Otis Jr.

What is Spiritual Mapping?

As the name suggests, **it is the mapping or the ability to read the spiritual forces behind the observable activities of our areas.** It is **Spiritual geography showing the routes and operations of the devil.** Again Spiritual Mapping is **an exercise of identifying demonic activities operating in an area.** Pastor Harold Caballeros of Guatemala City believes that spiritual mapping empowers intercessors in much the same way that x-rays serve physicians. In other words, spiritual mapping is the x-rays of a prayer warrior.

Engaging Spiritual x-rays

Engaging spiritual mapping x-rays is the process whereby intercessors use the readings of the invisible forces to pray targeted prayers. Spiritual x-rays are the forces that we see in the spirit though some of it may be coming from a natural happening.

Numbers 13:17-25

"When Moses sent them to explore Canaan, he said, "Go up through the Negev and on into the hill Country. See what the land is like and whether the people who live there are strong or weak, few or many. What kind of land do they live in? Is it good or bad? What kind of towns do they live in? Are they unwalled or fortified? How is the soil? Is it fertile or poor?

The above points us to the subject of spiritual mapping. It took forty days for the Israelites to finish the work of exploring the land. Whether God wanted them to do it or not is really not the issue. They saw the need and God authorized them to do so (Deuteronomy 1:22-24).

Spiritual mapping is an engagement process that requires a thorough investigation of the forces at work before we take them on in prayer. Spiritual mapping makes spiritual warfare easier.

Using **Numbers 13: 17-25**, Spiritual mapping can also be defined as **making a physical exploration of an area in order to discover the forces at work**. In Genesis 1: 2 we are told that; the earth was formless and empty, darkness was over the surface of the deep, and the Spirit of God was hovering over the waters. My principle is that, it is important to establish the present state of something before making any alterations or improvement. Discovery is the key to recovery. For example, if a pastor wants to pray for someone who desperately needs deliverance from demons, it is wiser for that pastor to establish the nature of the demons existing in the person before casting them out.

Purpose of Spiritual Mapping

Many people are committed to do spiritual mapping but nothing happens after that. In that way we cannot be effective. Spiritual mapping is always rooted in its purpose. If we do not know the purpose we lose the battle.

(a) To make Christians aware of the schemes of the enemy.

2 Corinthians 2:11

> *"In order that Satan might not outwit us. For we are not unaware of his schemes."*

The whole concept of Spiritual Mapping is based on the principles of being informed. **(Numbers13:26).** They came back to Moses and Aaron and the whole Israelite community at Kadesh in the desert of Paran. There they reported to them and to the whole assembly and showed them the fruit of the land. So whatever information our researcher discovers should be passed on to the body of believers. Awareness is the reason for this effective spiritual warfare

(b) For effective spiritual warfare.

Spiritual mapping precedes spiritual warfare. The whole essence of spiritual mapping is spiritual warfare. The Church must know that the purpose of spiritual mapping is spiritual warfare.

(c) To empower intercessors so that they can pray knowledgeably and fight properly.

Spiritual maping empowers intercessors and Christians so that they can best counter attack the spiritual forces of the enemy. Esther was empowered by Mordecai **(4:3- 17-5:10 ff)** and Esther took up her position before the king for the sake of the Jews. Mordecai also did the same.

How to get started with spiritual mapping.

(I) Organization and mobilization of manpower

Numbers 13:1 -2

> *"The Lord said to Moses, "Send some men to explore the land of Canaan, which I am giving to the Israelites. From each ancestral tribe send one of its leaders."*

The first step in spiritual mapping is organization and mobilization of leaders or a team of believers who can do the job properly. Not everyone qualifies for the work. It is advisable to take Spirit- filled believers to facilitate the gift of discernment during research. The team should be comprised of both men and women so that each particular areas of research can be taken care of. The spiritual maping team operates harmoniously under a special spiritual warfare unit. Special skills and gifts must be integrated together in such a way that will allow the full use of the potential and the application of good strategies.

(II) Praying together before making the move

The team must now come together for prayer to straighten their spiritual lines with the Lord. The team should exercise a high level of humility, Repentance and Prayer **(2 Chronicle 7: 14-15)**. People who are involved in spiritual warfare should seek the counsel of the Lord together **(2 Chronicles 18:4 - 5)**. Unless the Lord is with the team, they will do nothing. Whatever is born of prayer will certainly yield good results. So the team must start with prayer.

(III) Moving into an area to gather information

At this stage the team can now move out and start researching. The team can gather data in the following ways: -

(a) By observation of human environment and general behavior.
(b) By conducting interviews with people of the area.
(c) By reading media materials and artwork about the area.
(d) By listening to God in prayer.
(e) By looking at historical events of the area.
(f) By looking at the activities going on in the city.

After all has been done concerning research work, examine the distinction between primary and secondary sources. Primary sources are those which are uninterpreted e.g. census of the people, artifacts etc. Secondary ones are those that are interpreted, e.g. books, articles and dissertations etc.

Examples of research questions.

The questions should touch the spiritual, natural, material, health and historical aspects of the area. The questions should lead to something concrete that can be used in spiritual warfare.

The basic idea behind the questions is to know the forces at work in our areas. The following general questions are just some of the examples of the way to ask questions when conducting practical spiritual mapping.

- What percentage of the community considers itself Christian?
- Does there seem to be a genuine bond of unity among Christian Churches?
- What is the history of Church splits in the area?
- How visible is the Church in the area?
- What percentage of the community has been reached with the gospel?
- What is the most prevalent form of suffering in the area other than self afflicted pain?
- What are the evidences of family unity disintegration in the community e.g. Divorce, child abuse,
- What is the nature and extent of drug and alcohol abuse within the community?
- Are there a significant night clubs, disco houses, bars and beer halls.
- What serious physical or psychological side effects associated with new societal indulgences e.g. Aids HIV?
- Apart from Christianity what other major religions are represented in the community - e.g. Islam, Hinduism.
- Are pagan rituals or secular philosophies being practiced or encouraged in community schools? Are there secret societies operating in the community? (Masonic lodges, Witches, Wizards, Omen workers, Covens)
- Who are the most influential figures in the area?
- What other gods are worshipped in non Christian circles?
- Are there centers of idolatry and high places in the community?
- Who were the original settlers of the area?
- Are there any politicians, civic leaders or police officials who are going out of the way to obstruct the preaching of the gospel?
- What are the major killer diseases of the area and which age group is being affected by these diseases?
- Are people doing well in the community financially and physically?

Look at the situation of your area and ask as many questions as you can. There are so many questions to ask. The most powerful way of doing it is to assess the situation in the area both the positives and the negatives. Take into consideration the extent and nature of practices in the area. Look at some very consistent activities and the enemy within the gates. From here, build a series of questions to help you in solving the problem.

Factors Affecting Spiritual Mapping

1. Prayer and organization
Prayer must be the first thing and it should continue through out the research program. The team should be well organized and united. Prayer brings sensitivity and discernment in the group. It is from here that the group will get the mind of the Holy Spirit over what to do next. All spiritual mapping should begin here. Invisible forces can only be seen by spiritually prayer people.

2. Integrity of source

The prime interest here is determining the honesty and reliability of the person who gave the data. Look at the researcher's track record and check whether he/she has any vested interests. It is also important to recognize the difference between a statement of fact and opinion. Those receiving the information should not rush but scrutinize the data prayerfully. Not everyone can be entrusted with the work of research. Mature people should be trusted with this responsibility not just every believer.

3. Level of confirmation

Information must be treated with cautiousness. One source of information is not enough to create a platform for concrete conclusions. There should be other sources to allow a broader view of making conclusions. Consultations are very important. The most senior citizens of the area prove to be very reliable especially when looking at the history of the area. Two or three witnesses are better. Premature conclusions should be avoided.

4. Scriptural validation

This criterion rests upon one simple question: Does the fact conflict with the record or Principles of Scripture? If other materials are extra-biblical, it is better to handle them with caution and to test it carefully. But if there's conflict with scripture the only solution is to stop it and move on.

5. Readability

It is important that the information should be written clearly and plain (simple). It should accommodate the readers. It is a good policy to strive for brevity. So employ a good method of writing and presentation. Whatever is readable and accurate is worth looking at.

6. Contextualization

Every research demands its own context and the circumstances that govern the situation. A look at an area as it is very important in spiritual mapping. Information that is true of one area may not be true of a nearby area. Situations are totally different from one town to another. We must study each case separately.

7. Discernment

It's not every time that we can depend on historical facts and natural data. Sometimes facts may be there but the atmosphere in the spiritual realm keeps on changing due to several reasons and factors. A spiritual research team must be able to sense and discern the situation prayerfully. The Holy Spirit has his own way of revealing data about a particular area. What the Spirit of God is saying and showing us is of utmost importance and of greater concern. Both the results coming from discernment and natural research should be analyzed carefully to come up with the truth. For example, if you go in a very dirty city, research may tell you, 'this is the spirit of poverty,' Spiritual Discernment may say, 'these are demons of uncleanness and the spirit of negligence.' Having a complimentary account of all forms of research is a vital thing to do when researching about spirits.

Intercession and Spiritual Warfare

Intercession is another important dimension of spiritual warfare. Intercessors are a special task force in the army of the Lord. The Greek word used in the New Testament is, 'Enteuxis,' which means, **"a prayer with a set meeting time, place and purpose."** It also means, **to mediate or to stand in for another**. It is a free flowing, bold prayer which is prayed in faith. Another Greek word from the New Testament is 'Entuchano' which means, **"To fall in with, meet with in order to talk, to plead with a person with intensity of passion."**

The Hebrew concept of intercession is derived from two words...'Palah,' which means, 'to pray, to intervene, to mediate as a judge, to come between two parties.' The second word is 'Paga' which means, 'to encounter, meet with, reach or stretch unto, to entreat, to strike, to touch or to attack.' The etymology of intercession comes from the Latin word 'intercedere.' The word 'intercedere' is a compound word containing the words 'inter' and 'cedere.' Inter means 'to share with, in between, to meet, among, to stretch unto.' The word 'cedere' means, "to chance upon, to light upon, to judge with, entreat on behalf, stand in the gap, to face with."

The word 'intercedere' therefore means, 'to light upon in between, to stand in the gap with or to entreat on behalf of.''

True intercession can be defined as....

- **To entreat on behalf of other people**
- **To stand in the gap for others**
- **To mediate unto others**
- **The art of going in between**
- **To intervene/meet with God on behalf of another person**
- **To meet with through prayer**
- **To plead in prayer for other people**
- **To light or chance upon for other**s

From the above definitions four words can be used to sum up the concept of intercession. These are intervening, intercepting, interposition and interrupting.

One common feature in intercession is people. Intercession is not possible without people. The three people that make intercession are God, an intercessor and the people. An intercessor appeals or pleads to God on behalf of others (**Ezekiel 22:30**). Basically intercession is prayer offered on behalf of another. An intercessor fights on behalf of others. (Walter Wink says; **"History belongs to the intercessors."** "Intercession is more than an occasional heart warning, emotional love to God, more than expressions of goodwill on our knees. Intercession is an extension of the ministry of Jesus through His body, the Church, whereby we mediate between God and man for the purpose of reconciling the world to Him, or between Satan and humanity for the purpose of enforcing the victory of Calvary" (Dutch Sheats). Intercession is the responsibility of every believer – but that is not to say all believers have got the calling of intercession.

Portraits of Intercession

The progressive character of the divine leading of man is found in the development of the intercessory spirit. Sometimes we deal with the enemy more in intercession than in ordinary prayer. Christ intercessory prayer is the highest example and pattern of true intercession.

1. The intercession of Abraham for Sodom (Gen 23:33)
2. The intercession of Moses for water at Rephidim (Exodus 17:4).
3. The intercession of Samuel for Saul (1 Samuel 15:11).
4. The intercession of Christ for the believers (John 17).
5. The intercession of the Holy Spirit in fulfilling God's will in our prayers (Romans 8:26). The Divine Spirit is said to be the Spirit of supplication.

-   **Intercession plays a major role in spiritual warfare.**
-   **Intercession opens the gates of the enemy and releases the people into the kingdom of light.**
-   **Intercession builds the hedge in the battle for people to be saved.**
-   **Intercession will open the heavens for the Holy Spirit to move among nations.**
-   **True revivals are born in the womb of intercession.**
-   **Intercession penetrates the domain of darkness and sends signals of defeat to the devil.**
-   **Intercession provides a covering for the Church of the Lord Jesus Christ.**

True and great revivals are born in the womb of intercessory prayer

Prayer and Fasting

Every spiritual warfare encounter demands higher levels of prayer and fasting. All spiritual warfare involves praying but fasting changes the speed of things and heightens the levels of prayer and consecration.

What is prayer?

Prayer is to converse with God; the intercourse of the soul with God, not in contemplation or meditation, but in direct address to Him.

-   Prayer is "beseeching the Lord" (Ex. 32:11).
-   Pouring out the soul before the Lord" (1 Sam. 1:15). Praying and crying to heaven (2 Chr. 32:20)
-   Seeking unto God and making supplication (Job 8:5).
-   The art of drawing near to God (Ps. 73:28).

Prayer presupposes a belief in the personality of God, His ability and willingness to hold spiritual intercourse with us, His personal control of all things and of all His creatures and all their actions.

Acceptable prayer must be **sincere** (Heb. 10:22) and should be offered with **reverence** and **godly fear.** Prayer also requires a **humble sense** of our own insignificance as creatures and of our own unworthiness as sinners, with confidence as saints, with earnest importunity, and with unhesitating **submission** to the divine will.

Answers to prayer are determined by both our submission to God and our ability to believe Him

Prayer must be offered in the **faith that God is**, and is the hearer and answerer of prayer, and that He will fulfill His Word, "Ask, and ye shall receive" (Matt. 7:7, 8; 21:22; Mark 11:24; John 14:13, 14). Praying and believing is what brings answers in life.

- Prayer can be done in any of the following postures:
- Kneeling in prayer (1 Kings 8:54; Eph. 3:14).
- Bowing and falling prostrate (Gen. 24:26, Mark 14:35). Spreading out the hands (1 Kings 8:22, 38, 54; Ps. 28:2).
- Standing (1 Sam. 1:26; 1 Kings 8:14, Luke 18:11, 13).
- Sitting as well (Nehemiah 1:4).

Attitude and motive in prayer are more important than position and posture in prayer.

God answers prayer based on our attitude and our motive. If we accept the "Lord's Prayer" (Matt. 6:9-13), which is, however, rather a model or pattern of prayer than a set prayer to be offered up, we have no special form of prayer for general use given us in Scripture. So every prayer we pray is determined by our relationship with the Lord and our reason for offering that prayer.

Prayer is frequently enjoined in Scripture and we have very many testimonies that it has been answered. Men and women in the Bible who prayed in sincerity of heart and purity of motive always received what they asked from God. Examples below are a clear indication that God answers serious prayer.

- **Abraham's servant prayed** to God, and God directed him to the person who should be wife to his master's son and heir (Gen. 24:10-20).

- **Jacob prayed** and God inclined the heart of his irritated brother, so that they met in peace and friendship (Gen. 32:24-30; 33:1-4).

- **Samson prayed to God**, and God showed him a well where he quenched his burning thirst, and so lived to judge Israel (Judg 15:18-20).
- **David prayed,** and God defeated the counsel of Ahithophel (2 Sam. 15:31; 16:20-23; 17:14-23).

- **Daniel prayed,** and God **enabled** him both to tell Nebuchadnezzar his dream and to give the interpretation of it (Dan. 2: 16-23).

- **Nehemiah prayed,** and God **inclined** the heart of the king of Persia to grant him leave of absence to visit and rebuild Jerusalem (Neh. 1:11; 2:1-6).

- **Esther and Mordecai** prayed, and God **defeated** the purpose of Haman, and saved the Jews from destruction (Esther 4:15-17; 6:7, 8).

- **The believers in Jerusalem prayed**, and God **opened the prison doors** and set Peter at liberty, when Herod had resolved upon his death (Acts 12:1-12).

- **Paul prayed that the thorn in the flesh might be removed**, and his prayer brought a large increase of spiritual strength, while the thorn perhaps remained (2 Cor. 12:7-10).

"Prayer is like the dove that Noah sent forth, which blessed him not only when it returned with an olive-leaf in its mouth, but when it never returned at all."[23]

Prayer and fasting combined are the power of life. Prayer is talking or communication with God. Fasting is abstaining from food for spiritual purposes. Revivals are born out of prayer and fasting. Jesus began His ministry through prayer and fasting. It is interesting that the Holy Spirit led Him that way **(Matthew 4:1-3)**. The battle began immediately after the program of prayer and fasting. He had a shift from **fasting to fighting**. At the hills of great victories lie great battles.

Matthew: 17: 21

> *"But this kind does not go except by prayer and fasting."*

At every higher level of spiritual warfare, there are strong demonic forces at work. Prayer and fasting has got power to break through hardest domain of darkness. The devil and his demons cannot stand the power of prayer and fasting.

Acts 13:3

> *"So when they had fasted and prayed, they placed their hands on them and sent them off."*

Paul and Barnabas were commissioned after a great time of prayer and fasting. When the apostles had fasted and prayed, their spiritual senses became more active and they were able to hear the voice of the Holy Spirit.

The discipline of fasting teaches us much about our desires, our character and our values. **Isaiah 58:6 –12** describes the nature of true fasting. The Lord always regards that which is done right, with right motive and a pure heart.

---

[23]   By Robinson's Job

Isaiah 58:6-9

"Is not this the kind of fasting I have chosen: To loose the chains of injustice and untie the cords of the yoke, to set the oppressed free and break every yoke? Is it not to share your food with the hungry and to provide the poor wanderer with shelter - when you see the naked, to clothe him, and not to turn away from your own flesh and blood? Then your light will break forth like dawn, and your healing will quickly appear; then your righteousness will go before you, and the glory of the Lord will be your rear guard. Then you will call, and the Lord will answer; you will cry for help, and he will say: Here am I.

The above passage explains what true fasting can accomplish. Some of the results of fasting are as follows: -

- **Fasting deepens humility.**
- **Fasting increases the hunger for God.**
- **Fasting destroys the yoke of the enemy.**
- **Fasting solidifies determination.**
- **Fasting loosens the chains of injustice.**
- **Fasting sets the oppressed free.**
- **Fasting strengthens our faith.**
- **Fasting intensifies the prayer burden.**
- **Fasting breaks the stronghold of appetite.**
- **Fasting opens the heavens for God to pour out His Spirit.**
- **Fasting strengthens our foundation in the Lord.**

The Lord wants us to experience fasting in a right way **(Matt 6:18)** because there's a reward attached to fasting. The only warning that I can give to every reader of this book is – "do not use fasting as a tool of trying to force God to perform miracles for you." It is a distortion to think that God can only perform miracles after you have fasted. That's wrong. God can perform miracles with or without our fasting. Fasting is a discipline. Fasting should be treated largely as a self-humbling and self-discipline act. Fasting should be used mainly for consecration and seeking the Lord for His will to be done in our lives. It is here in fasting that, the Lord will show us greater and mightier things. Prayer and fasting plays a vital role in spiritual warfare.

Prophetic Actions

A prophetic action is a practical step done in faith and hope of what is conceived in the spirit. Prophetic actions can be done through banners, prophetic matches (Jesus Match), drama, Jesus film show, building of godly altars, songs of worship, spiritual demonstrations, and other portraits of the prophetic. The Lord led Ezekiel to the valley of dry bones **(Ezekiel 37)** and He asked him to speak prophetically to the bones. He spoke life into the bones.

Prophesying life into the bones at that time was prophetic picture of what the Lord was about to do to the nation of Israel. Jehoshaphat and his men began to sing songs of victory **(2 Chron 20:21-23)** before they could even encounter their enemies and the Lord gave them victory before they could start fighting. Moses stretched forth his rod on the water prophetically in great faith and the Lord gave him victory.

The Bible has a lot of prophetic actions that we can also use in our situations.

The 'Jesus Match' is a good portrait of a prophetic action. It releases the signals of defeat in the camp of the enemy. Worship dances are also a helpful tool in cleaning the heavens. Prophetic actions are not new to the Christian world. The only problem perhaps is that, many people do not take prophetic actions so seriously and some do not even understand what they entail.

A prophetic action is simply a practical demonstration with a specific hidden or open message whether by mouth or signs or words to demonstrate the desired destiny of a particular area.

For example, if we put a cross sign at the entrance of the city, we are saying: 'the city belongs to God, or 'this is a Christian city, or this is a home of believers' etc. At this point the cross sign has a prophetic hidden message for the good of the city. This serves the same way as banners.

A banner is an announcement and a pronouncement declaring something concrete to the people and to the spiritual forces in the heavens.

The power of prophetic actions in spiritual warfare…

- **Releases signals of fear and defeat to the camp of the enemy.**
- **Prepares the Church to possess the city**
- **Releases the atmosphere and cleanses the heavens from demonic activities.**
- **Disturbs the plans of the enemy**
- **Increases awareness and readiness.**
- **Brings the message of hope and victory.**
- **Makes the city respond to the Gospel.**

Praise and Worship

Praise and worship have got power to deal with the challenges of the enemy. Praise and worship are inseparable. These two are great weapons of spiritual warfare. This dimension of warfare is very damaging to the devil and to his demons.

Psalms 68:1

> *"May God arise, may His enemies be scattered; may His foes flee before Him."*

Psalm 149: 6-9

"May the praise of God be in their mouths and a double-edged sword in their hands, to inflict vengeance on the nations and punishment on the peoples, to bind their kings with fetters,

their nobles with shackles of iron, to carry out the sentence written against them. This is the glory of all his saints, praise the Lord."

The above scripture reveals the power of praise. Praise is a great weapon to stop the powers of darkness. The devil hates praise and worship. All praying in one way or another becomes praise because everything in life finds way into praise, the final consummating prayer. Another example is Jehoshaphat and his army.

2 Chronicles 20:21 – 22

"After consulting the people, Jehoshaphat appointed men to sing to the LORD and to praise him for the splendor of his holiness as they went out at the head of the army, saying: 'Give thanks to the LORD, for his love endures forever." As they began to sing and praise, the LORD set ambushes against the men of Ammon and Moab and Mount Seir who were invading Judah, and they wee defeated."

Praise knows how to attract and draw the presence of God. God delights in the praises of His people. Through the power of praise and worship, the Lord set ambushes against the enemies of Jehoshaphat. Praise and worship were David's secret of power in ministry. God still wants His people to worship Him. He is restoring the spirit of worship in the body of Christ. Praise and worship releases a great spiritual dynamism for God to do great things. The temple of Solomon was built out of gold and glittering substance. In short, it was a material temple. Herod's temple was a demonic altar of some kind. There was no reverence for God in this temple. Moses' tabernacle was functioning on the concept of law. And the truth is, we are not saved by law but by grace. The Lord is not any more interested in the material Church or the Church that is governed by law as it was with Moses. David's temple must be restored because it is time to sit as kings, seek the Lord and worship Him in the beauty of His holiness.

Acts 16:25 – 26

"About midnight Paul and Silas were praying and singing hymns to God, and the other prisoners were listening to them. Suddenly there was such a violent earthquake that the foundations of the prisons were shaken. At once all the prison door flew open, and everybody's chains came loose."

- Praise has power to break the chains of the enemy
- Praise and worship stops the missiles of the enemy
- Praise and worship attracts power
- Praise and worship
- Praise and worship is the key to loose the chains of the enemy.
- Praise and worship attracts God's presence

Deliverance and Evangelism

Deliverance and Evangelism happens to be the highest form of spiritual warfare at grassroots level. Deliverance has to do with releasing people from the power of demons or freedom from the dominion of the enemy **(Isaiah 61:1)**. Evangelism has to do with breaking through into the hearts and minds of the people to establish the rule of Christ in their hearts. In deliverance and evangelism, the focus is to rescue or save the soul of man which often entails fighting with the enemy.

Luke 4:18

> *"The Spirit of the Lord is on me, because he has anointed me to preach good news to the poor. He has sent me to proclaim freedom for the prisoners and recovery of sight for the blind, to release the oppressed."*

From the above scripture, we see two main aspects of Jesus' ministry while on earth. The first one being **evangelism (Preaching good news to the poor)** and secondly the ministry of **deliverance (Freedom, Recovery and Release)**. If the Church has to possess areas and cities for God, the key lies in the above passage. Evangelism and Deliverance must go together for an effective ministry. Demons are real, what makes a big change in spiritual warfare is to ensure that people are delivered from the oppression and yoke of the enemy. I will not exhaust the subject of deliverance as it has been already discussed in some parts of this book.

Evangelism or winning people to Christ should be the center of our spiritual warfare and all other spiritual activities. Winning people to the Lord is not an easy job as some people think. Many people are kept in the gates of the enemy. The Lord wants us to build the Church in the direction towards the gates of the enemy. This means that the devil has kept people locked up in his camp.

All we have to do as the Church of the Lord is to face these gates in prayer and evangelism, and take the people out of the domain of darkness through the deliverance ministry.

Any level of spiritual warfare that does not lead us to the ministry of leading people to Christ is of less value. We fight with the devil for one main reason – so as to allow God's will to be done on earth. We evict the devil in order to invite the Lord in.

The devil roars like a lion looking for whom to devour **(1 Pet 5:8)** but the Lord, the true lion of the tribe of Judah is seeking those whom He can deliver. Demons are not so much interested in staying in mountains as compared to their interest in people.

Demonology is very much biblical. To deny this fact is to give permit to the devil to oppress and trouble our people.

Most of the problems facing the world today are caused by demons. Today millions of people are bound living in poverty, oppression, obsession, fear, deception, sickness, idolatry and witchcraft. So if we just do spiritual warfare without delivering and evangelizing the people, many will still remain bound and lost. The end result of all spiritual warfare is to win people to Christ.

CHAPTER SIX

PRINCIPLES OF SPIRITUAL WARFARE

Maintain Your Spiritual Stand

Paul in Ephesians (6:14–17) discloses the spiritual armory of a believer that forms part of his stand in the Lord. The belt of truth is a protective belt against the lies of the devil. The breastplate of righteousness is a covering on our hearts to ensure that we practice righteous living. The sandals of peace are symbolic of our daily walk with Him and also that we are to prepare for battle by protecting our feet. The shield of faith represents our total trust in God and His Word rather than Satan and his lies. The helmet of salvation protects us from the blows of the enemy and it protects our minds. Finally we have the 'sword of the Spirit' which is the Word of God. It is both a defensive and offensive weapon. We resist Satan by the mention of the name of Jesus.

No backslider can fight the devil effectively. There is no power and protection outside the Lord. A right relationship with the Lord and a walk of righteousness are a must in spiritual warfare **(Proverbs 2:7).**

Victory cannot be achieved outside the Lord. One's stand in the Lord is the very first weapon in spiritual warfare. Jesus fought the devil from a position of knowing His stand in God. The following scriptures reveal this principle of spiritual stand....

1 John 4:4

> **".........**_He who is in you is greater than the one in the world."_

Psalm 11:3

> _".... If the **foundations** are destroyed what can the righteous do?"_

Dan 11:32b

> _".... But the people who know their God will do exploits and firmly resist the devil."_

Ephesians 6:10

*"Finally, my brethren, be **strong in the Lord** and in the power of his might."*

People Who Do Not Stand For Something Become Vulnerable To Demonic Attacks

The Church will only take possession of her inheritance by knowing her position in the Lord; Jesus fought the devil from a position of Him being the Son of God. We can best fight the enemy by taking our position in the Lord. This is the starting point in ministry. Spiritual warfare is for those with serious commitment and stand in the Lord.

Our stand in the Lord is the very first weapon in spiritual warfare. Every time we fight in spiritual warfare, we must fight from a position of knowing where we stand. Who we are is always the platform where we can defeat the devil.

Jesus in **John 8:14** faced His enemies because He knew where He was coming from and where He was going. He firmly declared His stand and destiny. He was not afraid. Another example is **Daniel 1:8,** he purposed in his heart not to defile himself with the royal food of the palace. He took his stand in the Lord. He was more concerned for his integrity in the Lord.

Whenever we lose our stand in the Lord we fall into the hands of the enemy. The devil is not looking for everyone to devour, he is looking for whom to devour. This shows that he has certain specific people in mind especially those who do not know where they stand and what they are doing. Our power in the Lord does not derive from what we do; it derives from who we are in the Lord. Nothing should be substituted for our stand in the Lord.

We are living in a world of changes and inventions. The absolute today can become the obsolete tomorrow.

There's always something special about keeping our fire burning and maintaining our stand in the Lord. The Word of God says, **"Those who stand or endure up to the end, the same shall be saved."** This means that, we must keep believing the Lord all the time and have His name on our lips at all time. If we stand firm in our faith and on our foundation, victory becomes possible and spiritual warfare starts from here. A person who has no stand in the Lord cannot fight the devil regardless of who he is and what he does.

A good example is **Acts 19:14 – 16;** the seven sons of Sceva who attempted to exorcise demons but unfortunately they lost the battle. The man with demons leaped on them and overcame them, and they fled wounded because the demoniac gave them a good beating. The sons of Sceva were overpowered even though they used the name of Jesus. The problem with the sons of Sceva is obvious. They never had a relationship with the Lord. They were leaning on nothing. The devil cannot stand a man who has a genuine stand in the Lord. Spiritual warfare is first a matter of relationship with Jesus. Relationship with Jesus is the key to use His name.

Just quoting the name of Jesus alone is not enough in spiritual warfare because many people today are using the name of Jesus in vain. No one can say; 'Jesus is Lord' except by the Holy Spirit **(1 Corinthians 12: 3)**

Our position in the Lord makes the difference and gives us a bold face when we are in the presence of the enemy.

The Psalmist says,

"The Lord is my shepherd, I shall no want," he further went on to say that; "even though I walk through the valley of the shadow of death, I will fear no evil; for thou art with me; thy rod and thy staff they comfort me. "These words can only be said by a man who is in relationship with God.

Psalms 125:1

> *"They that trust in the Lord shall be as mount Zion, which*
> *cannot be removed, but abides forever."*

Our strength comes from the position we have in the Lord. David faced the giant Goliath because he knew his position in the Lord. When we have our stand in the Lord, we can face challenges of any magnitude without fear.

Paul urged the Philippians **(Phi 4:1)** to stand fast in the Lord. We must not attempt to do spiritual warfare without knowing what our stand is in the Lord.

The Lord can only fight for us if we have a place in Him. Our position in the Lord is a position of victory because He who is in us is greater than the one in the world. So let's not lose our position.

Unification of Forces

Spiritual warfare requires higher levels of unity. The common saying 'united we stand, divided we fall' deserves no further explanation. Unification of forces entails partnership, unity, agreement, togetherness, spiritual fellowship and teamwork.

'It Takes a General to Bring down another General' (Clive Gopaul)

Acts 4:24

> *"When they heard this, they raised their voices together in prayer to God..."*

Exodus 17:12

"When Moses' hands grew tired, they took a stone and put it under him and he sat on it. Aaron and Hurl held his hands up one on one side, on e on the other – so that his hands remained steady till sunset."

Joshua 23:10

> *"One man of you shall chase a thousand, for the Lord your God,*
> *it is he that fights for you, as he has promised you"*

True Victories Are Secured In Teamwork

No one woman or man will win spiritual battles alone; it will take an army of the Lord. Partnership gives strength and victory in spiritual warfare. The devil always finds it easy to defeat one man but he has problems when it comes to the body of Christ.

Ecclesiastes 4:9

> *"Two are better than one, because, they have a good reward for their labor."*

V12

"A three fold cord is not easily broken"

A 'threefold cord' represents a solid environment; divine establishment and complete perfection. We cannot overcome the devil with independent and congregational visions. Unless we bring all our visions into the kingdom vision, victory is not possible. Two are better than one is a concept of unity. Spiritual warfare demands a great deal of unity, praying together, fighting together, sing together and move together. Teamwork brings power. Paul encouraged the Philippians to be **"one in spirit"** **(Phil 1:27)** and to pursue the common **purpose and goal**. The prayer of our Lord Jesus in **John 17** reveals God's desire for the oneness of His children. Doctrinal oneness may of course not be possible for obvious reasons.

Failure To Network In Combating Our Common Enemy Will Result Into Creating More Enemies.

Each believer today must begin seriously thinking on networking with others before they end up to be lovers of themselves.

Working as a Team Maximizes Our Potential to Overcome the Enemy in Shortest Possible Time.

Great results are maximized through teamwork and partnership. In teamwork, all the members work towards the same goal. In teamwork all different personalities come together with different backgrounds and agree to form a team to fight their opponent. The Church is a team of **'called out ones'** (the body of Christ) not just an independent Church with congregational mentality. Diversity should not be a scapegoat from unity. People should understand that there's diversity in unity. The human body is one but has many parts. All parts are supporting ligaments to ensure that the body does its work properly. The purpose of kingdom diversity is to fulfill every part and area the Kingdom of God. The other word is partnership. The word partnership comes from the word partner. As partners, you come into an agreement or a covenant relationship to work together and move together as one. The aspect of unity is a key to many blessings in the kingdom. Spiritual blessings demand a great deal of unity. Our Lord Jesus prayed a prayer of unity for believers **(John 17:21)**. It was His special prayer appealing to the Father in His passion for the unity of the believers. In this prayer lies one of the greatest secrets to living a life filled with the power and blessings of the Lord. The secret is that we may be **'one with God and one with one another.'**

Matthew 18: 19

> *"Again, I tell you that if two of you on earth agree about anything*
> *you ask for, it will be done for you by my Father in heaven."*

Where there's genuine unity, the sky is the limit to what the Church can do. A place of agreement is a place of unity. A place of unity is a place of power. The benefits of unity go beyond our scope. Though individual brilliance is required, it is the team that wins the game.

Psalm 133: 1 –3

"How good and pleasant it is when brothers live together in unity! It is like precious oil poured on the head, running down on the beard, down upon the collar of his robes. It is as if the dew of Harmon were falling on Mount Zion. For there the Lord bestows his blessing, even life forevermore."

God commands a blessing where there is unity. Unity brings the anointing of the Holy Ghost. In military, the army fights as a team. They go to war all of them prepared to fight the opponent. There is such a team spirit when they go together and that in itself builds them up to face the enemy without fear.

It seems today that the Church is just concerned with their independent ministries, each one on himself and for himself. The Lord Jesus cannot allow such a thing to continue in the Church – because it will limit the flow of the anointing on the body of Christ. Spiritual warfare needs a greater deal of unity and partnership. The "Body of Christ" is called 'the Army of the Lord' – which means, 'God's army.' He is the commander in Chief. As an army of the Lord, we are a united team ready to carry out the commands of our commander. The use of military language has a direct link to the type of war we are involved in and the nature of power we have. We cannot fight the devil without getting together as an "Army of the Lord." This is the best army so far.

Let us look at some of the benefits of partnership and unity.

- **Unity brings power (Matthew 18: 19)**
- **Unity brings blessings (Psalm 133:3)**
- **Unity brings protection (Beck. 4:10)**
- **Unity brings the anointing (Psalm 133: 2)**
- **Unity brings boldness (Acts 4:25)**
- **Unity brings victory (Matthew 18:19)**

- **Unity brings steadiness (Exodus 17:12)**
- **Unity brigs the glory (John 17:22)**

Genesis 11:6

> *'The Lord said, "If as one people speaking the same language they have begun to do this, then nothing they plan to do will be impossible for them."*

Unity requires one language, one mind and one purpose. One language is a way of saying 'we must confess the same message and hold one another.

According **to Genesis 11:6**, unity has got the potential to penetrate through the impossible realm. Unity is not just an agreement although agreement is part of unity. The Greek word for 'agree' (**Matt 18:19**) is *sumphoneo*. It means, **to be harmonious, to keep in accordance with, and to concur, to accord suitably.**

The biblical use of the word unity denotes something of quality not casual.

Our agreement in the Kingdom of God should be excellent and meaningful. Paul and Silas (**Acts 16:25**) entered into an agreement to praise the Lord in the midst of catastrophe. The Lord sent an earthquake or prison-quake to release Paul and Silas from the prison. This breakthrough came as a result of **unity, prayer and praise**. Unity plays a major role (**Matt 18:19**).

Knowledge of the Enemy.

Unless we locate the enemy we will never win the battle. In order for us to possess the gates of the enemy, we must focus our spiritual vision, locate the enemy, bind him and claim our territory. We cannot be effective in fighting with what we do not know.

Ignorance Is the Fastest Killer of Mankind

Ignorance always gives an opportunity for the devil to attack. Knowledge is a vital key to life. Possessing the knowledge of spiritual warfare involves the following areas of knowledge.

(1) Who is our enemy?
(2) How does this enemy operate?
(3) What are his activities?
(4) Where is the battleground?
(5) What is the strength of our enemy?

Christians must learn to assess the strength of the enemy.

We dare not go out against the power of Satan armed only with the man-made philosophies or inadequate spiritual resources.

Spiritual warfare is not for the blank minded believers. Some of the special areas of spiritual warfare are ……

- **The network of principalities**
- **Demonic strongholds**
- **Demonic altars and seals**
- **Characteristics of evil spirits**
- **Identifying the strongman**
- **Ancestral and territorial powers**
- **Blood covenants and sacrifices**

Matt. 12:29

> *"How can anyone enter a strong man's house and carry off his possessions unless he first ties up the strong man? Then he can rob his house."*

The Secret of Spiritual Warfare Is Always In Identifying the Strongman

Why do we need the knowledge of spiritual warfare?

- Knowledge makes us understand the enemy fully.
- Knowledge prepares us to wage war more carefully
- Knowledge defines our target more openly and clearly
- Knowledge uncovers the plan of the enemy
- Knowledge liberates us from fear and intimidation
- Knowledge closes doors of attack from the enemy because the enemy is identified before he attacks.
- Knowledge of the enemy brings confidence and boldness to attack the enemy.
- Knowledge of the enemy helps us to use our weapons correctly and rightly.
- Knowledge of the enemy gives us the key that we should use in preparing the strategy of attack against our enemy.
- Knowledge sends signals of defeat and fear into the camp of the enemy.

Learning about the devil does not mean to be devil or demon conscious. People who avoid lessons on the devil and demons are the ones who even become more prone to demonic and devilish attacks. A person who knows how the devil works will always avoid his tactics. Ignorance kills. The devil always takes advantage where there is ignorance. Knowing the devil and his schemes is always the key in defeating him.

Order and Obedience

(a) Order

The Spirit of the Lord is the Spirit of order. Our God is a God of order. Any military group that decides to go to war without order of some kind will produce a lot of casualties. The Church has produced casualties sometimes due to lack of order. An orderly atmosphere in spiritual warfare is a necessity. We cannot attack the devil with all sorts of confusion and disorderliness in our midst. In the Lord, we don't fight like the world does. Our fight in the Lord must be characterized by order. At the time of the fall of the walls of Jericho, there was an orderly arrangement of what was supposed to take place before the fall. Every one knew his part. The Church must attain higher levels of order. Spiritual warfare is not just a matter of fighting.

Organization and order are inseparable although the two are not the same. Where there's disorganization, people will eventually become disorderly. In organizations we select key fighting men, define their roles and station them. An organized army is a complete and prepared army with each soldier knowing what to do. Joshua's army was well organized and the rules were followed. Gideon's army was restructured by the Lord for the purpose of having an organized and genuine army **(Judges 3:1-2; 7:1-10)**. Spiritual warfare demands a higher level of organization. The army of the Lord is an organized army. We should know when to fight and how to fight.

Obedience

2 Corinthians 10:6

> *"... and we will be ready to punish every act of disobedience,*
> *once your obedience is complete."*

Psalm 81:13-14-

> *"If my people would but listen (obey) to me, if Israel would follow (obey) my ways,*
> *how quickly would I subdue their enemies and turn my hand against their fees."*

The Lord will use an obedient and organized army not just an army. The walls of Jericho **(Joshua 6: 1-16)** would have not fallen without obedience, order and organization. Before the priests could sound the trumpet, there was a series of instructions and a time of organization. Spiritual warfare must be instructional at times. When the Church of Jesus Christ gets organized and puts things in order, and carry out God's commands, victory and revival will break out without demonic resistance.

One of the strategies of the devil is confusion and disobedience. We have quiet a lot of Christians who are disorderly, and disobedient. This will cause the task of spiritual warfare difficult. Jesus fought the devil from a position of obedience to the will of the Father.

No Retreat – No surrender warfare

Jer 1:17

> *"Get yourself ready! Stand up and say to them whatever I command you.*
> *Do not be terrified by them or I will terrify you before them."*

Psalm 18:37

> *David says – "I pursued my enemies and over took them;*
> *I did not turn back till they were destroyed."*

Spiritual warfare is not for the weak **(Judges 7:1-5).** Once we engage the enemy in battle it's time to persevere and fight up to the end. There's no retreat in spiritual warfare.

The more we give up, the more the devil will have an upper hand on the people. For any Christian, giving up means defeat or loss. The moment we become afraid as children of God, scripture will work against us as God did say to Jeremiah.

A no retreat situation means – I will do what it takes to win the battle because it only makes sense that; the children of God should get the victory. God has designated victory for his children. Even when one knows that the devil will bring one attack upon another, giving up should be a no situation; hence it's a no retreat theorem in this sense.

In Spiritual Warfare, We Do Not Retreat We Only Entreat

The Holy Spirit never prevent us from the battles of life, instead he equips us for them **(Matthew 4: 1-4).** Allowing the devil to win the battle is a weakness on the part of the Church. This is because the devil has no grounds for winning the battle; he was defeated 2000 years ago. So my brothers and sisters don't give up! Keep fighting! Keep winning. The Church is destined to win. Nothing else can take the place of victory. This is why giving up is not in the vocabulary of Christians. Let me look at some of scriptures that will inspire courage and confidence in our hearts.

Hebrews 10: 35 – 36

> *"So do not throw away your confidence; it will be richly rewarded. You need to persevere*
> *so that when you have done the will of God, you will receive what he has promised."*

Number13: 30

> *"Then Caleb silenced the people before Moses and said, "We should go*
> *up and take possession of the land, for we can certainly do it."*

Luke 18:1

> *"Then Jesus told His disciples a parable to show them that*
> *they should always pray and not give up."*

Nehemiah 6: 11

> *"But I said, "Should a man like me run away? Or should one like*
> *me go into the temple to save his life? I will not go!"*

Nehemiah for sure was a strong man. Victory is for the strong, and for men of perseverance and determination. Spiritual warfare has not retreats. We cannot give up fighting spiritual battles. The Lord is the one who leads us in a triumphal procession. The devil was defeated 2000 years ago. All we need to do is to enforce the defeat. We must stand our ground and see the enemy flee.

2 Sam 22: 33 – 41

"It is God who arms me with strength and makes my way perfect. He makes my feet like the feet of a deer; he enables me to stand on the heights. He trains my hands for battle; my arms can bend a bow of bronze. You give me your shield of victory; you stoop down to make me great. You broaden the path beneath me, so that my ankles do not turn. I pursued my enemies and crushed them; I did not turn back till they were destroyed. I crushed them completely, and they could not rise; they fell beneath my feet. You armed me with strength for battle; you made my adversaries bow at my feet. You made my enemies turn their backs in flight, and I destroyed my foes."

A breakthrough is not total victory. What determines victory is the ability to destroy the enemy and fight up to the end. So if we are to stand firm up to the end, we have to fight. The Lord has not called us to a quitting life. David even though he was young was prepared to face the giant of his time. David knew no defeat in is vocabulary. The Lord wants us to fight and claim our territory. The gates of hell shall not prevail.

Matthew 11:12

> *"From the days of John the Baptist until now, the Kingdom of heaven has been forcefully advancing, and forceful men lay hold of it."*

There are two essential elements of the above passage.

(a) The Kingdom of God has been forcefully advancing.
(b) Forceful men lay hold of it.

The word advance means, motion towards, approaching something, violent move. This is a concept of Kingdom advancement. Every ministry must think of Kingdom advancement. Forceful men are men of stamina, with spiritual violence and strong determination.

Forceful men are fighters fit for a fight. No matter how the devil may try to intimidate us, we should not be afraid of him. Our role is to possess. Let us stand like the three mighty men of David **(2 Sam 23: 8 – 12)**. One of them was Shammah who stood his ground when all Israel ran away. He took his stand in the middle of the field to defend the field. He defended it and struck the Philistines and the Lord brought about a great victory. The Lord always works with men who are prepared to fight the enemy.

Discipline

Heb 12:7-8

> *"Endure hardship as discipline; God is treating you sons for what son is not disciplined by his father. If you are not disciplined (and everyone undergoes discipline), then you are illegitimate children and not true sons."*

V 13

> *'No discipline seems pleasant at the time, but painful later on, however it producers a harvest of righteousness and peace for those who have been trained by it.'*

Discipline is one of the expensive traits in the Kingdom of God. The biblical meanings of the word discipline are as follows: -

Chastisement, reproof, warning, instruction, also restraint, to check, correction, rebuke, and doctrine.

All the above renderings entail something important in spiritual warfare.

Chastisement: This is God's method of maturing and pruning His people. It is punishment of some kind. It is indeed very painful. The purpose of God's chastisement is cleansing and growth. Chastisement refines us to be God's holy vessels.

Reproof: Process of guidance and test to seek the best out of us. It is here that God shows us our mistakes so that He can prove us better. Reproof and rebuke are relative terms. This also applies to the word correction. The key word in attaining the Lord's discipline is willingness to accept correction. The Lord reprimands us or rebukes us to correct us and to direct us to what is right. Rebuke in most cases leads to warning. Following every correction is a warning. To be a disciplined army we must take the Lord's warning and listen to his rebuke. Reproof, rebuke and warning are sub components of correction. The Lord will always reveal what are our weaknesses are so that His strength can be made perfect in us. The area of rebuke is the most avoided area of ministry by many people. It takes some amount of humility to accept correction and rebuke.

The term **'to check'** implies self-evaluation and analysis. This is a discipline issue. The army of the Lord must constantly do spiritual check ups. I like this part of discipline because it reveals our weaknesses and strengths. To check ourselves is to ensure that our spiritual inventory is done. Today's absolute is this microwave society can become tomorrow's obsolete. It is therefore required for the army of the Lord. To do constant check ups. The battle lines are tense today than before. So we must count the cost by checking ourselves thoroughly.

Instruction: Instructions here refers to specified guidelines and a set of reliable and corrective information, discipline also entails the ability to instruct someone in the way he / she should go. The Word of God is full of instructions for believers to follow. We need to possess strict adherence to these instructions. The Lord's instructions are the best. In each situation, the army of the Lord must be guided with special instructions depending on the context of the situation.

Doctrine – Doctrine and instruction are closely related but the two cannot be taken to be the same thing. Instructions are always a set of guidelines. Doctrine is the summation of The Bible truth. It is the description of the truth found in The Bible. This shows that we must know the doctrine we profess or the beliefs we have. In every doctrine there are instructions. The army of the Lord should not believe everything and anything anyhow. Any wrong doctrine will hinder us from advancing further.

The army of the Lord should attain higher levels of discipline and determination.

Spiritual warfare is a discipline on its own. It will therefore take people who are fully disciplined to get involved. In the natural, military discipline happens to be the highest level of discipline. Military discipline is inescapable and irresistible. If military discipline in the natural is of great value, why should spiritual discipline become so cheap? Our Lord Jesus Christ expects us to attain higher levels of spiritual discipline. Though painful, discipline is strength. It has value and for reaching benefits.

Hebrews 11:24

> *"Moses chose to suffer afflictions with the people of God*
> *than to enjoy the pleasures of sin for a season."*

Moses chose in other ways to endure hardship as discipline with the family of God than to settle for perishable things of the world.

Most of the Israelites could not enter the Promised Land because they failed to cope up with God's disciplinary tests. The Lord will never allow us to fight the enemy without first of all equipping us **(Judges 3:1-3).** Only those who have been disciplined of the Lord will be able to face the ferocious beast called devil and conquer his kingdom in the power of the Almighty God. If the Lord was to deliberately stop disciplining his children, the Kingdom of God will produce the greatest number of casualties than ever before. Many will be hospitalized. Carelessness is a result of no discipline in many cases.

Other important areas of discipline are

- **Discipline in the way we handle kingdom resources.**
- **Discipline in relationships with others.**
- **Discipline in our working places**
- **Discipline in domestic issues, husband, wife and children.**
- **Discipline in public and community issues.**
- **Discipline in political matters.**

All these areas provide us with the potential to either defeat the devil or to be defeated by the devil depending on how we handle each particular area of discipline. Now is the time to get a disciplined army of the Lord that will quench the fiery darts of the devil.

Anointing of the Holy Spirit

Jesus fought the devil in the power of the anointing. The Spirit of God was upon Him to deal with any situation of the enemy (Isaiah 61:1-6; Acts 10:38). A generation of the anointing will not stay under pressure. During creation, the Holy Spirit was moving upon the surface of the water to deal with every level of darkness. It is indeed not by mighty nor by power but by the Holy Spirit **(Zechariah 4:6-8).** We are dealing with the world of principalities and demonic powers. Only the Holy Spirit power can face and extinguish the demonic powers. Fighting the devil without the help of the Holy Spirit can be disastrous and dangerous. Praying according to the will of God is only possible by the Help of the Holy Spirit. No wonder Paul says, 'pray in the Spirit in all occasions at all time.' Some of the characteristics of the Holy Spirit in Spiritual Warfare are:

- **The Holy Spirit Breaks the yoke of the enemy (Isaiah 10: 27).**
- **The Holy Spirit will raise a standard against the devil (Isaiah 54:17)**
- **The Holy Spirit will level down the strongholds of the enemy (Zechariah 4:6 – 8)**
- **The Holy Spirit will expel darkness in every place he goes (Genesis 1: 2)**
- **The Holy Spirit releases the prisoners (Isaiah 61:1-3)**
- **The Holy Spirit empowers the believer to pray effectively (Romans 8:26 –27)**
- **The Holy Spirit removes fear of the enemy (Romans 8:15)**

The power of the Holy Spirit is able to handle any situation and any level of battle that we can encounter in spiritual warfare. The Holy Spirit can penetrate any city and any nation of the world at any time. The Church must move in the power of the Holy Spirit in all her spiritual battles. The devil cannot stand the power of the Holy Spirit.

CHAPTER SEVEN

EXPOSING AND ARRESTING LUCIFERIAN SYSTEMS

Satanic schemes uncovered

The greatest challenge in this fast and furious world is that most people fail to see who really their enemy is. Satanic schemes are methods and tactics that the devil uses to get people off the Lord.

(1) Getting people busy with life

The devil works through the process of activities. He gets hold of every opportunity he finds to distract people from what they truly need. One way he does this is by making people busy bodies. A lot of people have been made busy by the enemy such that they have no time to pray, no time to spend with their kids, no time to spend with their spouses. By the time some people knock off from work, they are tired and they break down easily. His whole plan is to get people focused on non essentials of life.

(2) Giving people flashy and glittering life

Today, TV is one force where the devil maximizes the temptation of making people wander off from the Lord. The devil's plan is to occupy homes with wrong movies and by doing so; he is robbing people of what they truly need in life. This world has become pleasure and luxury driven. The devil's strategy is to make people spend more on entertainment as a way of distracting them from gaining hold of their saviour.

(3) Getting people buried in issues.

We all have issues to deal with in life but it is never the intention of our maker to get us lost in our issues. God created man and gave him dominion. If man's focus is God, then all his burdens and cares will be taken care of. Newspapers and magazines have created a major shift in the world of information. Showbiz reports, soccer highlights, and Hollywood highlights are getting people focused on wrong issues. These issues end up depressing and destroying families. Other issues are family issues such as division and quarrels specifically designed by the enemy to make families dysfunctional.

(4) Giving people what they want.

The devil is always looking for the ground where he can sow his seeds. The easiest way he does this is by giving people what they want. Nowadays, the devil doesn't have to guess to know what people want. He knows people want speed, so he gives them fast cars. They want entertainment, so he gives them nude beaches and all the sex movies. People want freedom, so he gives extra marital affairs to adults and rebellion to their children. The devil is constantly knocking on the mind of man to confirm what next is he or she looking for. Man is tempted by his own desires of the flesh but it is the devil who delivers the goods in different packages.

Luciferian Operations

Everywhere, the devil operates with structures and through people. He knows that his time is short and he is pregnant with a mission of stealing, killing and destroying life. Because of his six thousand years advantage over man, he has gained experience and expertise on how to operate effectively. Here below are the vital points on how Lucifer operates.

- **He works through people and situations**.

The devil visited Adam and Eve unexpectedly and through the situation they had with God, he devised quick means of launching his attacks on humanity. He takes advantage of the arrangement God had made with man over the tree of life. He changes the configurations and through Eve, he managed to score points over Adam and Eve. He is still doing the same thing even today. He takes hold of existing situations of the people and launches his attacks directly or through weaker vessels.

- **He works through organizations**

Organizations both religious and non religious are potential platforms for achieving maximum results. The devil recognizes this truth. He takes special interest in certain firms, institutions, and companies that he can work through. Some companies facilitate satanic activities in the name of charity. Shopping malls are built by organizations that have made great sacrifices to Lucifer. He works through schools and institutions of learning. Some Children instead of getting better, they worsen after completing varsity.

- **He works through politics**

Politics can be transformed for good or better. The political arena is one vehicle that is highly strategic in getting to masses of people at one time. Some politicians are not as many people think they are. They are placed in places of rulership to effect Lucifer's bid for world control. The devil picks key influential people to get into the hearts of many. If those involved in politics are not careful to watch what they do and say, their lives will start going down slowly.

- **He works through ungodly policies**

The devil works much through policies and decisions at governmental level. In most secular societies, abortion is legalized constitutionally and now one can find placards in street walls saying 'abortion 100% safe and painless.' Some States in the USA have authorized gay marriages and same sex marriages. There is a huge drift in values and ethics in our current societies. People have become lovers of money and creators of evil. Many good cultural norms have been compromised in exchange with secularization. Through governmental or national laws such as constitution, the devil has gained an upper hand setting up his operational structures in the earth.

- **He works through Churches and pastors.**

Not every Church is a God fearing Church and not every pastor is truly called by God. Some Churches are just a means through which Satan can deceive many innocent followers. Some churches are centers of false worship and breeding grounds for demonic and satanic activities. I do not want to state names but I tell you there are so many satanic and false churches around. They mention the name of Jesus quiet well but they do something else of their own.

Demonic and Ungodly Establishments

Another challenge that is very central in spiritual warfare is the establishments of areas and structures dedicated to foreign gods. These establishments come in different sizes and forms and they serve as centers of attraction. Traditional healers, witch doctors, magicians, brothels, escort agencies, sex clubs, adult shops are all demonic establishments.

These establishments are part and parcel of the society so long people are comfortable. Herebelow is what these establishments do to people in the society:

- They provide temporal satisfaction
- They lift up the desires of the flesh in people
- They transfer demonic spirits on people (masturbation, lust, sickness, rebellion on those who take part in them).
- They create demonic images in the minds of innocent people.
- They establish seeds of the enemy in people.
- They steal people's precious time.

People go to demonic establishments because they seek satisfaction but little do they realize that these same establishments have grave consequences. The consequences of these establishments are:

- They invite rebellion
- They cause people to become unfaithful
- They produce heaviness in the end
- They cause family division
- They cause addiction to people
- They blind the minds of the people
- They lead to death
- They bring terminal sicknesses
- They destroy people's dignity and identity.

The devil always presents the wrong thing in best packages. He decorates sin giving it a shinning view making people wanting it more and more. Once he creates a platform to convince people that what they are doing is fine, he adds more lucrative baits to hook people to his tunes. For example, people are highly cautioned about the danger of smoking but they still want to smoke; people know the risk and danger of having extramarital affairs but they still insist on doing it; people know the consequences of telling lies but they still want to tell lies and so forth. They do this because they have been hooked by the devil

Demonic structures in government systems

If there is an area of operation where the devil would like to exercise much control over the people, the government is that area. The devil functions effectively through structures and through strategic people. Given the choice, the devil would like to work with people such as doctors, teachers, engineers, soldiers, policemen, businessmen, clergymen, scientists and political leaders. All these people or professions have choices to either serve the people faithfully or to become a means through which the devil can achieve his mission. Governments operate with structures that are operated by people. Because of the love of money, cultures of corruption, cultures of discrimination, cultures of violence, cultures of theft, cultures of poverty have become major prime time stories on TV. Once these cultures settle in the nation, Lucifer unleashes his missiles all over the nation and he begins to spread other levels of wickedness in the nation. This is what brings the nation totally down. If righteousness exalts the nation (Proverbs 14:34), then wickedness drowns the nation (Proverbs 14:11). When the nation closes the ear to the things of God, the devil builds an embankment around that nation. Perhaps the scripture below will shade some more light on why recognizing God is important in the nation.

Luke 19:42 – 44 (World English Version),

"If you, even you, had known today the things which belong to your peace! But now, they are hidden from your eyes. For the days will come on you, when your enemies will throw up a barricade against you, surround you, hem you in on every side, and will dash you and your children within you to the ground. They will not leave in you one stone on another, because you didn't know the time of your visitation."

The devil often times gets into governments through policies, laws, and enactments. Having a constitution that legalizes abortion is just another form of sacrifice and murder. Allowing gay marriages or same sex marriages is another form of perversion. Legalizing prostitution is simply destroying the value of humanity. Governments are about structures and systems. All the devil does is to take advantage of these structures by using people within the same structures. Demonic systems are established in governments when political leaders subscribe to things that are not right in the sight of God. Most of the demonic systems enter governments through the following opportunities.

- International agreements
- Political scandals
- Initiation ceremonies involving government officials
- Parliamentary bills
- Amendments of statutory laws
- Decision making bodies
- Sacrifices and dedications

This generation is not the only generation to have problems with demonic structures. Demonic structures were there in Babylon, in Egypt, in Jerusalem, in Ephesus and many other places. The difference with our time is that, men and women of God in Bible times were very decisive and confrontational in dealing with the enemy. Daniel when he was in Babylonian captivity refused to defile himself with the royal food.[24] He knew that the structures were contaminated. Moses when he had grown up refused to be called the son of Pharaoh's daughter. He chose to suffer affliction with the people of God than to enjoy the pleasures of sin for a season.[25]Esther she refused to stay quiet after realizing that Haman was planning to kill the Jews. The Christians took their stand and disagreed with the program of the enemy.

Dethroning demonic authorities and systems

Thank God that even when all the demonic activities and authorities are advancing to take over the earth, the Church of Jesus Christ is being prepared to be a light the shines in darkness. Being light is the only calling that darkness cannot oppose. Jesus came into this world as 'the light' of the world and everywhere He went, He shined with spiritual light in the hearts of men. There is no argument between light and darkness as to which one should go first. The presence of light demands that darkness go.

Governments for now may seem to be flourishing and gaining upper hand on the people. Politicians and world leaders may look like they don't need the Church but that's not it. What happened in Babylon and Egypt can still happen today. Pharaoh systems were disintegrating and the man Pharaoh was failing to find sleep. The magicians and the stargazers could no longer use their powers. The wise men were running out of ideas and time was running out for Pharaoh. Same thing happened to the Babylonian kings. Nebuchadnezzar's men could not read nor interpret the dreams of the king (Daniel 2:10-11; 4:7). In short, kings, their powers and systems were failing to sustain their kingdoms. In both stories, it took the voice of the Church or righteous men to restore blessings on the Kingdom. Egypt needed a Joseph and

---

[24]   Daniel 1:8
[25]   Hebrews 11:24 - 25

Babylon needed a Daniel. Today, the whole world needs a Saviour and His name is JESUS! The Church will always triumph no matter what politicians do or say. God's business cannot be conquered by human affairs. To dethrone authorities and demonic systems, believers must engage the following practical steps.

(a) Pray strategic prayers.

It is impossible to penetrate government demonic systems and thrones (authorities) without the language of prayer. Men and women of God in old times shaped their world by engaging strategic and earnest prayers. Elijah was one man but through earnest prayer stopped the rain for three and half years and he loosed the rains again in the land. Daniel prayed three times a day. Joseph while in Egypt prayed to God. Moses did the same. Jesus prayed while here on earth (Hebrews 5:7). The apostles in the early Church prayed earnestly and they wrought great wonders. They shook communities for God. They overtook the religious systems and turned the world upside down.

(b) Positioning of believers in right places.

Daniel or Joseph after knowing what was happening around them could have easily walked out on Nebuchadnezzar and Pharaoh respectively. They did not do that. They stayed right in there. They worked from the inside. They served evil kingdoms faithfully and did not allow themselves to be contaminated. Joseph, Moses, Daniel and Esther all knew that the effective way of overcoming authorities and demonic systems is to work from the inside. If you are a Christian and you are working in a company full of unbelievers and wicked bosses, don't stay out of there. Stay in there unless God is telling you to move. You are the light the company may be waiting for. The earth is truly groaning for the revelation of the true sons of God. People stay in darkness because the light has not shined on them. Some ignore the light but the truth is; light cannot be ignored. The example of Esther is a motivation on how Christians should position themselves even in risky situations. We cannot dethrone demonic systems by running away from them.

(c) Partnering with others in building Godly patterns.

It is impossible to overthrow demonic systems by doing things independently. Daniel shared the request with his friends so they could together seek the mercies of God (Daniel 2:17 – 18). Moses partnered with his brother Aaron in seeing that, the mission was a success. Though some people in the Word of God may seen to have fought the battle single handedly, the fact is, they were not alone. Esther was not alone because many Jews were fasting for her. Joseph was not alone because God's angels and his father were making intercession for him. It is when we are united that we can easily dethrone demonic systems.

(d) Patience in serving the governmental systems

We cannot overcome demonic systems if we are in a hurry. Demonic foundations and evil structures take years to establish themselves in places or in people. Daniel after testing the lion's den would have simply walked away for fear of the worse to happen. He came out of the lion's den and still continued to serve the same king who put him there. Joseph after testing the prison would have simply walked away but he did not do that. He went back to serve the same system. Even in heaven, there is no sticker that says; "those who want overnight transformations, apply here." The secret to God's power is timing.[26] If we are to deal with the demonic structures of our society, we need to be very patient in waiting upon the Lord to unleash His strategies for us to use.

(e) Praise the Lord who does mighty things.

Praise is always a powerful weapon of spiritual warfare. If you follow through the words of Daniel, those of Joseph, those of Moses and the Israelites; you will realize that they all praised God by openly acknowledging what God was going to do or what God had done. Jehoshaphat knew the power of praise when he assigned musicians to the front as they were facing the Ammonites and Moabites.

2 Chronicles 20:21-22 (Standard Version).

And when he had taken counsel with the people, he appointed them that should sing unto Jehovah, and give praise in holy array, as they went out before the army, and say, Give thanks unto Jehovah; for his loving-kindness [endureth] for ever. And when they began to sing and to praise, Jehovah set liers-in-wait against the children of Ammon, Moab, and mount Seir, that were come against Judah; and they were smitten.

---

[26]   Dr. Reginald Wilson Sr, FGMI, Marrero, LA, USA.

CHAPTER EIGHT

STRATEGIC AND CONFRONTATIONAL WARFARE

Spiritual warfare demands strategy and confrontation. A strategy is a plan of how we can go about doing something. The Word of God contains dynamic principles of attacking the enemy and possessing the kingdom of darkness effectively. Every section of evil must be confronted without fear. The weapons we have contain divine power to demolish every stronghold of the enemy. Strategic and confrontational warfare has the following characteristics.

Facing the Enemy

We cannot engage the enemy and then fail to confront him and face him. Running away cannot help; we've got to take our stand and face the devil.

Jeremiah 1:17

> *"Get yourself ready! Stand up and say to them whatever I command you.*
> *Do not be terrified by them, or I will terrify you before them."*

Jeremiah received a go ahead word from the Lord to fight against the kings of Judah. He had no option except to go. The Kingdom of God needs forceful men (Matthew 11:12). Some people have landed themselves into more trouble by failing to face the enemy. The more one hides from his/her enemy the greater the possibility to increase the enmity between the two. We cannot live together with the devil and let him attack our families openly and kill innocent people. We have to face him in prayer and combative intercession. Jesus had to face the devil head on until he ensured total victory over the works of the enemy (1 John 3:8b). He disarmed all the principalities by the death He died on the cross. The same anointing which was in Jesus is in us today. He is the one who leads us into triumphal procession. So we can confidently face the enemy with an overcoming spirit. The Lord is with us in this battle. The battle belongs to him. There is nothing to fear at all. The only way we can defeat the evil one is by fighting him in the power of the Holy Spirit.

Offensive Warfare

The Bible contains much of offensive spiritual warfare than defensive warfare. One of the reasons why sometimes we lose battles is we are more on the defensive side than the offensive side. To be offensive is to launch an attack straight on target. Many Christians do not understand the difference between defensive and offensive spiritual warfare. To ask the Lord to protect us from fear and slumber is defensive warfare.

To rebuke and destroy the spirit of fear and slumber in prayer is offensive warfare. This unlocks the key to offensive warfare. Jeremiah was set apart by the Lord to destroy and to tear down the works of the enemy **(Jer 1:10)**. Jesus came to destroy the works of the enemy **(1John 3:8b)**. The gates of the enemy are keeping people locked up and held captive; the Church must move towards the gates of the enemy, break them and advance inside to take people out of bondage. The Lord Jesus is building the Church towards the same direction. The Lord has given us the keys of the Kingdom to open and lock doors **(Matthew 16:18 -19)**. In this warfare, we use more of the offensive weapons than defensive ones. David pursued his enemies **(2 Sam 5:19)** to make sure that he had total victory.

Psalm 18:37-38

> *"I pursued my enemies and overtook them; I did not turn back till they were destroyed. I crushed them so that they could not rise; they fell beneath my feet."*

We will never win the battle by sitting idle waiting for the Lord to give us everything on a silver plate. A good offense is always the best defense. The Church must learn to attack. The Kingdom of God is all about kingdom advancement. We have to **be forceful**, **vigilant** and **aggressive**.

God's Demolition Squad

God's Demolition Squad is a group of Holy Ghost filled believers who are devoted to intercession, prayer and spiritual warfare for the purpose of demolishing and extinguishing demons and satanic powers. The three mighty men of David are a good example of God's Demolition Squad.

2 Samuel 23:8-12

"These are names of David's mighty men: Josheb, a Tahkemonite, was chief of the Three; he raised his spear against eight hundred men, whom he killed in one encounter. Next to him was Eleazar son of Dodai the Ahohite. As one of the mighty men, he was with David when they taunted the Philistines gathered at Pas Dammin for battle. Then the men of Israel retreated, but he stood his ground and struck down the Philistines till his hand grew tired and froze to the sword. The Lord brought about a great victory that day. The troops returned to Eleazar, but only to strip the dead. Next to him was Shammah son of Agee the hararite. When the Philistine banded together at a place where there was a field full of lentils, Israel's

troops fled from them. But Shammah took his stand in the middle of the field. He defended it and struck the Philistines down, and the Lord brought about a great victory."

This is an interesting passage on warfare. It is a good example of what I call God's Demolition Squad (GDS). You can imagine the whole Israeli army fled but David's mighty men remained to fight the Philistines. These men were just like us, very ordinary but with extra - ordinary determination. What makes the above passage so interesting is that, each of the three mighty men had a specific battle to encounter. The last part of the passage says, "the Lord brought about a great victory." This indicates that the three men were not fighting in their own power but the strength of the Lord. The battle was divinely approved but there was need for the three men to be strong and to fight. Josheb killed eight hundred men in one encounter. This is unbelievable and beyond human understanding. Think about it - one man to kill eight hundred fighters with a spear in one encounter. This is a clear indication that, the three men were anointed of the Lord to fight great battles. No size of an army can overcome the strength of the Lord. Even today, the Lord is prepared to use us in the same way even much greater. The Lord Jesus gave His disciples authority over all the power of the enemy **(Luke10: 19)**. The Church needs mighty men of faith with strong spiritual fighting muscles. To be able to wage big battles, one must be highly trained and fearless. We have a situation in the Church today where no one is willing to fight greater and dangerous battles. We are lacking front liners. One man cannot kill eight hundred men unless he knows the person behind his power and how to rightly use the sword. Churches must develop the habit of training people in strategic spiritual warfare. David himself was a fighter. He killed the giant of his time Goliath. No one was willing to face Goliath in battle. David trained his three men in the same way and he probably passed on his fighting anointing to his men. These men were not depending on the arms of flesh. All they knew was - God was on their side. The Lord is always in favor of His fearless and obedient servants.

Disarming the Enemy

The enemy (the devil) and his demons must not be underestimated or taken for granted. The devil and his demons are highly skilled and specialized in most of the activities of the world today. The devil possesses a great deal of knowledge in all areas of human sphere. He knows all the nations of the world, he knows how to do politics, he knows how banks operate, he knows Churches very well, and he has data of every accident that takes place in the world. The list is endless when it comes to the operation of his kingdom. So we must render the devil powerless and useless through the God given authority. Our Lord Jesus made it easier for us by disarming the devil at the cross.

Colossians 2:15

> *"And having disarmed the powers and authorities, he made a public spectacle of them, triumphing over them by the cross."*

We must not give the devil the opportunity to attack us. The Church must be united in all areas of the ministry to allow a greater anointing upon the Church.

The weapons of our warfare are not carnal but mighty with divine power to pull down every stronghold of the enemy. The Church must be equipped in every area of spiritual warfare. Areas of weakness and ignorance will become potential areas of our future defeat. Any area of ignorance on the part of the Church gives the devil an opportunity to attack. Scripture offers us with one hundred percent assurance of victory over the enemy. He who is in us is greater than the one in the world. In other words, the God in is greater than the devil. So let us forge ahead to possess what is legally ours with fear.

Seizing the Victory

The battle belongs to the Lord where as the victory belongs to the upright. This is to say that, in every battle we face in life, it is the Lord who fights for us not ourselves; and because the Lord is not a loser, we have the victory with us everyday. The Lord told Moses that, 'the land where your foot shall tread on I give it to you.' This **rhema** word kept Moses going. God through His precious promises has given us the victory. All we need is to seize the God given victory through prayer and trust in the Nothing shall harm us at all. The battle is the Lord's does not mean we should sit idle and let the Lord do everything for us. The Lord Has given us the ability to produce wealth but it is our responsibility to work hard and maximize our usefulness here on earth. To stay lazy is to remain poor. Seizing the victory sounds so nice but it comes by hard work.

Certain steps must be applied for us to assume victory.

(a) **Putting our trust in the only true God.**
(b) **Walking in obedience to God's Word at all times.**
(c) **Confess positively and always give thanks to God.**
(d) **Engaging the enemy in battle through prayer.**
(e) **Knowing that we are the head not the tail.**
(f) **Walking in practical faith.**
(g) **Walking in righteousness.**
(h) **We must be involved in serving the purposes of God.**

The above points will usher us in the realm of the God given victory. There is no need for us to fear the devil because he was defeated 2000 years ago. The Lord wants us to overcome the enemy for it is Him who leads us in a triumphal procession. So we need to take the victory despite the intensity of our warfare.

The Jericho Warfare

Spiritual warfare operates at different levels. It differs from one place to another. Principles are the same all round. The story of Joshua and the walls of Jericho is a good example of high and strategic warfare on how to take cities for God. This kind of warfare is tough and difficulty to encounter. In this kind of warfare, we need to hear God properly. A look at the following scripture will highlight us more on this kind of warfare.

Joshua 6:1-5

"Now Jericho was tightly shut up because of the Israelites. No one went out and no one went in. Then the Lord said to Joshua, "see, I have delivered Jericho into your hands, along with its fighting men. March around the city once with all the armed men. Do this foe six days. Have seven priests carry trumpets or rams' horns in front of the ark. On the seventh day, march around the city seven times, with the priests blowing the trumpets. When you hear them sound a long blast on the trumpets, have all the people give a loud shout; then the wall of the city will collapse and the people will go up, every man straight in."

The above passage contains a series of instructions that are important in spiritual warfare. In Jericho kind of warfare, we must possess the determination to march around the walls of our cities and nations through the power of prayer. Joshua was given instructions by the Lord of how to take the city for God. Let us look at some of these key principles.

(a) See, I have delivered Jericho into your hands - vs 2

Whenever we are possessing areas for God, we must first of all get the assurance of what is divinely given to us. The word **'see'** speaks **of vision, perception, focus, sight and sensitivity.** We must already begin to see victory before we can even attain it. People who see the invisible can do the impossible. The Lord wanted Joshua to perceive the victory in the supernatural realm before he could do anything in the natural realm. As far as God was concerned, Jericho was given to Joshua. The battle must be won first in the spiritual realm before it is captured in the natural realm. The Lord wanted Joshua to rest in the Lord's victory. In spiritual warfare, there's no need for us to be in panic because Jesus defeated the devil on the cross. All we need to see is victory.

(b) March around the city once with all the fighting men. Do this for six days- v 3

The demonstration of the victory that was earned and perceived in the spiritual realm began here when all men started marching around the walls of Jericho. It was one step at a time for six days. It took a lot of strength, faith, courage, and boldness to march around the city. This was a prayerful march.

Whatever they discerned each day, they possibly dealt with it at the camp in prayer. It is a wonderful principle to notice in warfare that, we must be acquainted with the city to effectively discern the spirits of the city but we must be with God in the closet to destroy the spirits or demons of the city. Only the Lord can give us the power to overcome. The battle belongs to the Lord.

(c) Have seven priests carry the trumpets of rams' horns in front of the ark - v 4

here was need for complete involvement of front liners and key leaders to sound the trumpets of victory. The leaders must be in the fore - front to announce and to declare victory in the spiritual ream. People began to lift up the name of the Lord through the sound of the trumpets. On the seventh day, they marched with intensity and persistence seven times. The seven priests sounded the trumpets; the people marched around the walls boldly. The number seven speaks of completeness and spiritual perfection. It shows that the battle was not premature. It was timely and divinely approved, the men were well prepared and everything was in its place to ensure total victory for the Israelites. Greater battles often establish principles that solve lesser battles. To fight every battle is to raise the level of things of lesser importance to a greater significance than they deserve and this inevitably sends confusing signals. Moses was able to use what he had in his hands. This time the priests are required to blow the trumpets.

(d) ...have all the people give a loud shout - verse 5

The maximum point of the victory came when all the people gave a victory shout. They all lifted up their voices in at one time upon hearing the sound of the trumpet. They shouted only after all was done. We should always shout where the Lord wants us to and be quiet where there's need for us to be quiet. Shouting as the last thing to do after all have been done is the best way of ending the battle. Even in prayer meetings, it is important and advisable to start with the prayers and end with shouts of praise. This is just a good advice, it is not a must. All fighting men after going round the walls of Jericho concluded the battle with shouts of victory. It was after the shouts that the walls of Jericho collapsed and every man went straight in to possess. Shouting for no reason is a waste of time.

It is good to shake cities but God has called us to take cities.

Strategy for city transformation

The ultimate end of all spiritual warfare is to build the Church of God and to possess the gates of the enemy. Secondly, spiritual warfare must lead us to city transformation. Every pastor must understand that, to take the city for God, there must be a strategy good enough to transfer people from the kingdom of darkness into God's Kingdom.

Second Chronicles provides us with a good strategy for a genuine city transformation.

2 Chronicles 17:3-10

"The Lord was with Jehoshaphat because in his early years he walked in the ways of his father David had followed. He did not consult the Baals but sought the God of his father and followed his commands rather than the practices of Israel. The Lord established the kingdom under his control; and all Judah brought gifts to Jehoshaphat, so that he had great wealth and honor. His heart was devoted to the ways of the Lord; furthermore, he removed the high places and the Asheral poles from Judah. In the third year of his reign he sent his officials Ben-Hail, Obadiah, Zechariah, Nethanel, and Micaiah to teach in the towns of Judah. With them were certain Levites -Shemaiah, Nethaniah, Zebadiah, Asahel, shemiramoth, Jehonathan, Adonijah, Tobijah and Tob Adonijah - and the priests Elisa and Jehovah. They taught throughout Judah, taking with them the book of the law of the Lord; they went around to all the towns of Judah and taught the people. The fear of the Lord fell on all the kingdoms of the lands surrounding Judah, so they did not make war with Jehoshaphat."

The above passage offers us with every strategic step of taking the cities for God. There are four main strategic steps to city transformation.

1. Seek the Lord - verses 3-4, 6

Jehoshaphat began a transformation process by establishing a relationship with the Lord as it was with his mentors. He entered into a covenant relationship built on righteous and godly principles. In short, he began with God seriously. This was the foundation for his future victory. He put fellowship and relationship with the Lord first **(Dan 11:32b; Jer 9:24; Matt 6:33)**. We must always begin with the Lord in order to do big things for him. Jehoshaphat began to walk uprightly with before the Lord. City transformation cannot come by having a powerful conference or a revival meeting of some kind. Well and good if it does. The very first thing is, believers of the city must enter in a covenant relationship with God. This is where it all starts. The Church of the city must be encouraged to seek the Lord and to live right.

2. Destroy all demonic altars of the city - v 6

The Bible says, "Furthermore, *he removed the high places* and the Asheral poles from Judah." This is the work of every Christian in every city, to ensure that all satanic objects are destroyed. The Church should not tolerate demonic altars, high places, disco houses, occult thrones, brothels, bars and drinking places etc. The foreign gods of the city must be brought down. The Church must exercise the God given authority by bringing down the idolatrous altars in prayer. Believers should be the first to condemn all devilish activities and demonic centers of the city. Jeremiah was anointed of the Lord firstly to uproot, to tear down, to destroy; and then to build **(Jer 1:10)**.

The process of removing these demonic altars involves: -

(a) Identification of demonic activities of our city

The Church should be able to do effective spiritual mapping and identify potential sites for demonic activities. Guess work is not enough. Nothing should be hidden from the sight of the Church. Intercessors should closely monitor the activities of the city together with the pastors so that the whole Church can be fully informed. Banners and posters to condemn every immoral act should be produced all over the town so that community can know that the Church wants a clean society. All demonic altars should be brought down. We should use every possible means of stopping the works of darkness. Believers should take deliberate steps to stick positive and biblical quotations specifically to condemn demonic forces at work in our city. This is a fighting stage.

(b) Confrontation (Matthew 11:12; 12:29)

The Bible urges us to bind the strongman first before we can take his goods. Strategic prayer, intercession and spiritual warfare should be offered in confrontation with the enemy. We must confront all demonic forces without fear.

3. Select and mobilize leaders - v 7 - 8

Jehoshaphat mobilized different ministries into a network to facilitate team ministry for city transformation. The leadership anointing must always be there where change has to take place. Jehoshaphat knew very well that he needed officials, priests and pastors to carry out the strategy. Most of our strategies for city transformation fail to work due to lack of key and reliable leaders. Another reason is lack of kingdom network. Key leaders must be in the forefront. This is a facilitating stage. All gifts should come together and serve the kingdom vision.

4. Teach God's Word to all people in the city - v 9

The preaching of the Word of God is one of the major keys to city transformation. The strategy of Jehoshaphat is a great commission concept because its mandate to teach the word to all mankind (Matthew 28: 19 -20). People must hear the word for them to believe the Son of God. Jehoshaphat used a three-step process of reaching the communities with the word. The leaders were mobilized already. Now came the time to make disciples through....

(a) Corporate Evangelism

All the leaders were committed to preaching the Word of God. There was a corporate anointing for evangelism. There was unity of function. It was not a one man's job. The people of Judah were hit by the good news of the kingdom. The early Church began the same way.

(b) Clear Emphasis of the Word

Teaching the Word of God (The book of the law) became the chief duty of everyone. The Word of God kept on going through from house to house. None was left out. The city can only change by constantly emphasizing the preaching the Word of God without comprise. We certainly have the world to reach; to stop the preaching of the Word of God is to delay the coming of the Messiah. Every city needs the Word of God daily not just a revival meeting.

(c) Confrontational Evangelism

Every sinner big or small must be confronted with the gospel of the Lord Jesus because the gospel is the power of God unto salvation. The rich and the poor must all hear the word without favoritism. None should be spared when it comes to the Word of God. The Word of God is for mankind regardless of one's status in the society. This is time to gather the lost sheep. There is more room in the kingdom for sinners to come in. If we faithfully use the four strategic steps, we will certainly take our cities for God. Remember God has not called us to shake cities; He has called us to take cities.

What next:

After what you have gone through in this book, I urge you to pause and start asking God to cloth you in His armour. You are not the only one going through the challenges you are encountering in life. Rise up in the spirit of a warrior, fight in prayer and conduct yourself in the manner worthy of the Lord. Now this world, not having the light of God, is entirely in spiritual darkness, and demons reign in it; for God is not there-except in supreme power after all, turning everything to His glory, and, in the end, to the good of His children. So build yourself up in prayer and claim your victory through the power of Him who triumphed over all the power of the enemy. Do not allow the god of this world to blind your mind (1 Corinthians 4:4).

References

Arnold, Clinton E. 1997, *3 crucial questions about spiritual warfare*, Grand Rapids: Baker Books.

Billheimer, P, 1996, *Destined for the Throne*, how spiritual warfare prepares the bride of Christ for her eternal destiny, Minnesota, Bethany House Publishers.

Cerullo, M, 1996, *God's Victorious Army, Financial breakthrough and spiritual warfare Bible*

Douglas J.D, & Rev Norman, 1982, *New Bible Dictionary* (Completely revised and reset).

Duewel, Wesley, 1986, *Touch the world through prayer*, Grand Rapids, Asbury books.

Eastman, D, 1991, *No easy road, inspirational thoughts on prayer,* Grand Rapids: Baker Books.

Fucius, J, 1995, *The Powerhouse of God* - 'The Statement to the world of principalities and to powers'

Garrison, M, 1980, *How To Conduct Spiritual Warfare As I See it.*

Jacobs, Cindy, 2001, *Deliver us from evil.* Ventura, CA: Regal Books.

Mostert, B, 2000, *Change your World Through Prayer.*

Murphy, Ed, 2003, *The handbook of spiritual Warfare*, Nashville: Thomas Nelson Publishers.

Ortis, G, Jr, 1993, *Spiritual Mapping Field Guide*, the Sentinel Group.

Strobell, L, 2000, *The case for Faith, a journalist investigates the toughest objections to Christianity.* Grand Rapids: Zondervan.

Thomas, N, 1997, *The Nelson (NKJV) Study Bible*, Nelson Thomas Inc.

Wagner, P, 1991, *engaging the enemy*, Ventura: Regal Books.

Wagner, P, 1992, *Warfare Prayer*, Ventura: Regal Books.

Watchman, N, 1970, *'Sit, Walk, Stand'*